BEHIND THE TENT FLAPS

#773

Ex Libris

Donated by
Ruth Slander
In memory
of Edna
James

The Church of Christ
North Canton, Ohio

Stephen T. Wyatt

Behind the Tent Flaps

What You Never Heard But Need To Know About Marriage

COLLEGE PRESS PUBLISHING COMPANY • JOPLIN, MISSOURI

Copyright © 1997
College Press Publishing Company

Printed and Bound in the
United States of America
All Rights Reserved

Cover design by Daryl Williams

All Scripture quotations, unless indicated, are taken from
THE HOLY BIBLE: NEW INTERNATIONAL VERSION®.
Copyright © 1973, 1978, 1984 by International Bible Society.
Used by permission of Zondervan Publishing House.
All rights reserved.

Certain products mentioned by name in the text are used for illustrative purposes only and should be understood as the registered trademarks of their respective companies. Neither endorsement nor criticism of these products should be inferred.

Library of Congress Cataloging-in-Publication Data

Wyatt, Stephen T. (Stephen Thomas), 1955–
    Behind the tent flaps: what you never heard but need to know about marriage/Stephen T. Wyatt.
    p. cm.
    Includes bibliographical references.
    ISBN 0-89900-788-0 (pbk.)
    1. Married people in the Bible. 2. Married people—Religious life. 3. Marriage—Religious aspects—Christianity. I. Title.
BS579.H8W93 1997
248.8'44—dc21   97-19153
                                                    CIP

To Vanessa:

It seems hard to believe,
but we've shared a tent for two decades now.

You know me best, yet love me most.

I love you.

Table of Contents

Introduction 9

1. Living with One You Don't Love 15
    Genesis 29–30

2. Wounds from Sticks and Stones Heal Better 33
    Genesis 12:10-20

3. Sticking Together When Life Falls Apart 55
    Job 1–2

4. One Night of Ecstasy, A Whole Lifetime of Agony . . 77
    2 Samuel 11–18

5. Lust Is a Many Splintered Thing 99
    Judges 13–16

6. When Your Faiths Don't Mate 121
    Exodus 4:21-26

7. He Who Dies with the Most Toys — Still Dies . . 141
    Acts 5

8. My Daughter Married a Workaholic 171
    Exodus 18

9. When You've Married a Short Fuse 191
    1 Samuel 25

10. The Way Things Ought to Be 213
    Genesis 2:18-25

Introduction

A noted Christian author received a letter from a woman who had moved, along with her new husband, into a small apartment. After they moved in, they noticed a troubling noise from above the ceiling and realized someone else also called that apartment home. It was a *mouse!*

Now this woman could tolerate a lot of things, but a rodent was not one of them. So her beloved hubby busied himself with the task of mouse removal — he set baited traps and then waited for that inevitable SNAP! Sure enough, in a couple of days, they had nabbed their uninvited house guest.

The trouble is, the trap didn't kill the mouse — it just wounded him. And not wanting to just kill him *"in cold blood,"* they put the mouse — trap and all — in a bucket of water (thinking that the most compassionate way to dispose of the poor fella would be to drown him). Not willing to witness his struggle, they left the house for a while. When they returned, they were shocked to discover that the mouse was still alive — struggling for all he was worth, delicately balancing himself on the top edge of the trap, and straining just enough to keep his tiny nose a fraction of an inch above the water line.

The woman didn't say in her letter what they did next —

because the mouse wasn't the point of the letter. The point of the letter was her need to admit the following:

> *"My marriage has been like that mouse for many years — and I feel like I've been standing on one aching toe with my nose just barely out of the water."*

I wonder how many other couples feel that same way? How many mates are disappointed because life in the home hasn't turned out the way we thought it would? How many husbands and wives live in grinding discouragement because our marriage is not all we had hoped for? And yet, clinging to the hope of what might still be, we keep straining and stretching with all that is in us — to survive, to hold on, to endure yet another day.

I don't know who it was who coined the phrase, but it's just not true. Your marriage was not made in heaven. *The institution itself was.* But your particular relationship? That has to be forged out between you and your partner here on earth. And while it is true that God is the Author and the Designer of the marital union, we are His contractors. He called it into being from the throne room of heaven, but the maintenance work is up to you and me.

And it doesn't take a rocket scientist to realize that we're not doing very well. If you don't believe that, the next time someone in your workplace announces wedding plans, just listen to the response. Don't talk, just listen. More often than not, the bulk of what you hear will be a mixture of snide remarks and sarcastic put-downs. Why, you'd think the poor guy had just announced plans to move to Siberia!

And what about those who are already married? Just think of the couples you know who, not even three years ago, seemed happily married — but now? They're either divorced, or they are living totally separate, disconnected lives.

Fred Smith, a Christian businessman from Texas, once asked a prominent psychiatrist what percent of American marriages are happy ones. He said, *"Less than 25 percent."* What was the test he applied? *"Both partners would gladly do it over again,*

Introduction

knowing what they know now about each other." He said most married people think they could have done better . . . and would if they had it to do over.

Shelly Winters, not exactly a novice at getting married, admitted what all of us have observed:

"In Hollywood all marriages are happy. It's trying to live together afterwards that causes all the problems."

Another wit has described marriage as a three-ring circus: First you have the engagement ring, then comes the wedding ring, and finally you get the suffering!

Funny words, I suppose. But our laughter sounds hollow, even forced. Because it's not just in Hollywood. The breakneck decline of modern marriage can be found in every town and village, in every neighborhood and, dare I say it? Even in every church. And even the most casual observer is beginning to wonder if the so-called, happily-married couple even exists! It's almost to the place that you wonder if God's words that **"it's not good for the man to be alone"** (Gen 2:18), really ought to have read, *"it's not good for the man to be married."*

The scene is bad, people. Real bad. *But I wonder if it wouldn't help, even just a little bit, to realize that it's **never been** perfect?* At least not since the day Adam and Eve got booted from the Garden. Ever since that fateful day, marriage has been anything but a tip-toe through the tulips.

And I'm so thankful that God has been faithful to let us see that. I'm so glad that the Bible is not just a compilation of naive idealisms or idyllic fantasies, describing some blissful experience that simply does not square with reality. I'm really glad that the Bible honestly reveals life as it was . . . and is.

That's what this book is all about. This book is an honest look at marriage as it has always been. You see, the typical temptation is to glamorize the men and women of the Bible — with the sad result that we make them appear far more saintly and angelic than they really were. Because that's the way we like our heroes. Strong and free from any obvious weakness or frailty. The trouble is, that's just not the way it was. As you'll discover in this book — some of the greatest of your biblical heroes occasionally floundered in their marriages.

Problem is, no one ever told me that. So I imagined my heroes enjoying wonderfully idyllic relationships. And then I wondered, *"Why is it that they could pull it off, but I'm struggling?"* I know now that they struggled too. It was then that I decided it was high time someone take a straightforward, honest, behind-the-scenes look at some of God's most famous couples. Couples who struggled, just like you and me.

And you know, somehow I think it will help us just to know that. Perhaps just knowing that Abraham and Sarah had a problem with verbal abuse, or that Samson struggled with a roving eye, or that Moses was a workaholic, or that David had to fight back from a devastatingly adulterous relationship — maybe just knowing that will help us be a bit more realistic when it comes to our own relationships.

Because the truth is: THERE IS NO SUCH THING AS AN IDEAL MARRIAGE. There never was, and there will never be. I know, it's easy to see that couple two rows in front of you on Sunday morning and assume that, because they appear to have it together, they, in fact, have marriage wired. I'm telling you right now, *they do not.* Oh, there are some basically happy couples to be sure, and there are other couples who have adjusted to one another quite well and who enjoy an amazingly harmonious relationship — but they struggle, just like you, just to keep their noses out of the water!

Maybe your Sunday School teacher never told you, but I'm telling you now: Not even the greatest heroes of Scripture were free from marital heartache. And because I feel it so essential that you know that — this book is written as a straight-from-the-hip, gutsy look behind the tent flaps of some of God's greatest. And I promise: *I'll tell you everything I find — warts and all.* And I really believe it's going to help a lot of people. No, I have no delusions of marital perfection for you or me or anyone else — but I *am* absolutely convinced that the princi-

Introduction

ples outlined in this book can result in an amazing transformation in your home.

So grab a cup of coffee, kick back in your favorite reading chair, and dig in. And as you draw back the tent flaps on these famous people, you might want to whisper a prayer of thanksgiving that the Word of God is no longer being written. Because if it were, who knows? Your story would probably raise a few eyebrows, too. Just like Jacob's.

CHAPTER ONE

Living with One You Don't Love
GENESIS 29–30

Pat Williams, current General Manager of the Orlando Magic basketball team, a number of years ago faced what was, in his view, the greatest challenge of his life. Pat thought he had a *good* marriage: His wife was beautiful, talented and a good mother. She was, in short, everything Pat could have wanted. The trouble is, Jill felt that she meant nothing more to Pat than the *little woman who handled everything at home so he could soar in his career.* For years she had tried to get his attention, but to no avail. Finally, after ten years, she had had it. On a cold December Sunday, she said, *"Pat, I just don't love you anymore. Of all the places in the world, I would rather be any place but here. I will stay with you for the sake of image,"* she said, *"but my love is dead."*

What did Pat do? Well, what do you do when you don't love the one you're with? What do you do when the one you're with doesn't love you? I'm asked those questions quite a lot. More than I care to recall, quite frankly. And most who ask me those questions are church people. Christians who are not necessarily besieged by enormous, monstrous problems — and yet, the feeling is gone. The love seems dead. And what they want to know is: WHAT DO YOU DO WHEN YOU DON'T LOVE THE ONE YOU'RE WITH?

JACOB AND LEAH:
An Honest Look At A Loveless Union

Well, before I share with you what Pat did — I want you to understand that a loveless marriage is not a new phenomenon. It certainly is not an invention of modern America. Quite honestly, it's as old as Scripture itself. In Genesis 29, one of the great patriarchs of Israel, Jacob, son of Isaac, arrives in Paddan Aram for the purpose of seeking a wife. In obedience to his father's warning against marrying an unbeliever, he traveled to this region in order to find a mate from among his mother's people. The first person he met was Rachel, the daughter of his mother's brother, his uncle Laban. And there was an instant connection between the two. We don't know if it was love at first sight, but we do know that:

> "After Jacob had stayed with him for a whole month, Laban said to him, 'Just because you are a relative of mine, should you work for me for nothing? Tell me what your wages should be'" (Gen 29:14b-16).

> "Jacob was in love with Rachel and said, 'I'll work for you seven years in return for your younger daughter Rachel'" (Gen 29:18).

In other words, after knowing Rachel only 30 days, he was ready to marry her. Laban saw this as a very good business deal, so he readily agreed.

> "Laban said, 'It's better that I give her to you than to some other man. Stay here with me.' So Jacob served seven years to get Rachel, but they seemed like only a few days to him because of his love for her" (Gen 29:19-20).

Doesn't that sound like a line from some mushy romance novel? Anyway, Uncle Laban pulled a fast one on Jacob. On the night of his wedding, instead of giving Rachel to Jacob, he slipped in his older, much less attractive daughter, Leah, instead. Verse 16 explains:

> "Now Laban had two daughters; the name of the older was Leah, and the name of the younger was Rachel. Leah had weak eyes, but Rachel was lovely in form, and beautiful" (Gen 29:16-17).

> **"But when evening came, he [Laban] took his daughter Leah and gave her to Jacob, and Jacob lay with her"** (Gen 29:23).

I don't know how Laban pulled that off. Maybe Leah wore an extremely heavy veil, and since the ceremony was at night, Jacob had no idea until it was too late. Or maybe Laban spiked the punch bowl and Jacob was so blasted, he had weak eyes, too! Either way, Leah obviously knew what her father planned. Was she a willing participant? Did rivalry with her sister enter into the equation? We simply don't know. We do know that once she was in the marriage, she expected to be treated as a full wife and not an afterthought.

Can you imagine Jacob's horror, when he awakened the next morning and it was LEAH?! At first, he probably did a double-take. Or maybe he thought, *"Momma told me women aren't as pretty in the morning, but this is ridiculous!"* Then it hit him: *"This isn't Rachel — it's Leah!"* And he bolted right out of that tent, headed straight for his father-in-law, and said,

> **"'What is this you have done to me? I served you for Rachel, didn't I? Why have you deceived me?' Laban replied, 'It is not our custom here to give the younger daughter in marriage before the older one.'"** [We just don't do things that way around here.] **"'Finish this daughter's bridal week; then we will give you the younger one also, in return for another seven years of work'"** (Gen 29:25b-27).

And so he did. And as far as Jacob was concerned, 14 years was a small price to pay for the love of his life.

> **"He finished the week with Leah, and then Laban gave him his daughter Rachel to be his wife. Jacob lay with Rachel also, and he loved Rachel more than Leah"** (Gen 29:28b,30a).

However, all was not well in this home. *It never is when love is missing.* There are a number of battles these three encountered — but let me mention only two:

First, was the battle of **INSECURITY**. When you're not loved — and you know you're not loved — all sense of stability is removed. And far too often, in a desperate attempt to earn love, things are done in hopes that the unloving partner will take a second look. In Leah's case, she tried to earn Jacob's love through childbirth, which, by the way, is *never* a good idea.

"When the LORD saw that Leah was not loved, he opened her womb, but Rachel was barren" (Gen 29:31).

So obviously, Leah saw this as her chance to grab the spotlight.

"Leah became pregnant and gave birth to a son. She named him Reuben, for she said, 'It is because the LORD has seen my misery. Surely my husband will love me now'" (Gen 29:32).

When that didn't work . . .

"She conceived again, and when she gave birth to a son she said, 'Because the LORD heard that I am not loved, he gave me this one too.' So she named him Simeon" (Gen 29:33).

When that didn't work . . .

"Again she conceived, and when she gave birth to a son she said, 'Now at last my husband will become attached to me, because I have borne him three sons.' So he was named Levi" (Gen 29:34).

When that didn't work . . .

"She conceived again, and when she gave birth to a son she said, 'This time I will praise the LORD.' So she named him Judah. Then she stopped having children" (Gen 29:35).

I give up! It's not going to work! Love just isn't in the cards for me!

Another battleground was **JEALOUSY**.

"When Rachel saw that she was not bearing Jacob any children, she became jealous of her sister" (Gen 30:1a).

In fact, much of chapter 30 is a description of a seething female sibling rivalry for the affection of one man — and the battle was waged in the bedroom. When Rachel couldn't have children, and knowing that Leah was running a baby factory over in her tent, she decided to give Jacob her maidservant, and she bore him a child. Not to be outdone, Leah gave Jacob her maidservant. And then Leah changed her mind, and had two more sons herself — and then finally, even Rachel had two sons. It was ridiculous! Twelve kids were born! Simply because Jacob didn't love Leah.

*Now it's my conviction that he could've **learned** to love her.* That's what his daddy did. Isaac didn't even get to see Rebekah until after the ceremony was over. It was an arranged marriage from beginning to end — and Isaac wasn't even consulted. And yet, Genesis 24:67 says, "Isaac brought [Rebekah] into the tent, and he married [her], AND HE LOVED HER." Note that: It doesn't say that Isaac dated Rebekah and fell in love with her and then they got married because of their romantic attachment. It says that he brought her into the tent, he married her — and *then* he loved her!

And that's one of the principles we need to learn. Love is not primarily an emotion of the heart. LOVE IS AN ACT OF THE WILL. The love our world sings about is nothing more than an involuntary response to external stimuli — it's like falling into a ditch. You can't help it; it just happens.

You've heard the songs:

"Some enchanted evening,
You may see a stranger,
You may see a stranger
Across a crowded room
And somehow you know,
You know even then
That somewhere you'll see her again and again."[1]

Isn't that amazing? You show up for a dinner party and whamo! Your world is turned upside down, and you've fallen helplessly in love with a total stranger! You didn't mean to, it just happened!

That's what Elvis believed. He crooned that familiar refrain, *"I can't help falling in love with you."*

The Doors belted out their own version of helpless love: *"Hello, I love you, won't you tell me your name?"*

Behind the Tent Flaps

But that's not true love. At least not ALL of love. Certainly emotion is a *part* of love. We have all experienced the rush of infatuation. Every one of us knows the joy of a pounding heart and accelerated breathing and wobbling knees. And it's wonderful, it's exciting, it's stimulating — but that's not *all* of love. It's not even the CORE of love. True love, abiding love — the kind of love that sustains a home — is a much deeper love than mere animalistic passion.

In the musical, *Fiddler on the Roof*, Tevye, after many years living with Golde in an arranged marriage, finally musters the courage to ask,

TEVYE: *"Do you love me?"*
GOLDE: **"Do I what?"**
TEVYE: *"Do you love me?"*
GOLDE: "Do I love you?
    With our daughters getting married
    And this trouble in the town,
    You're upset, you're worn out,
    Go inside, go lie down.
    Maybe it's indigestion."
TEVYE: *"Golde, I'm asking you a question —*
    Do you love me?"
GOLDE: "You're a fool."
TEVYE: *"I know —*
    But do you love me?"
GOLDE: "Do I love you?
    For twenty-five years I've washed your clothes,
    Cooked your meals, cleaned your house,
    Given you children, milked the cow.
    After twenty-five years, why talk about
    Love right now?"
TEVYE: *"Golde, the first time I met you*
    Was on our wedding day.
    I was scared."
GOLDE: "I was shy."
TEVYE: *"I was nervous."*
GOLDE: "So was I."

Living with One You Don't Love

> TEVYE: *"But my father and my mother*
> *Said we'd learn to love each other.*
> *And now I'm asking, Golde,*
> *Do you love me?"*
> GOLDE: "I'm your wife!"
> TEVYE: *"I know —*
> *But do you love me?"*
> GOLDE: "Do I love him?
> For twenty-five years I've lived with him,
> Fought with him, starved with him.
> Twenty-five years my bed is his.
> If that's not love, what is?"
> TEVYE: *"Then you love me?"*
> GOLDE: "I suppose I do."
> TEVYE: *"And I suppose I love you, too."*
> Then together they sing:
> *"It doesn't change a thing,*
> *But even so,*
> *After twenty-five years,*
> *It's nice to know."*[2]

You bet it is. And that's the kind of love — not the ooey-gooey, warm-fuzzy, slurpy kind of love — but the committed kind of love that lasts. The kind of love that Isaac learned to have for Rebekah. And the kind of love that Jacob — had he been so disposed — could have learned to have for Leah. But because he chose the lesser path, his home was marked by insecurity, jealousy, unhappiness, and, perhaps worst of all, grinding loneliness. Mother Teresa says that loneliness and the feeling of being unloved are the greatest poverties in the world. And I think she's right.

Interestingly, Jacob tried to fill his poverty by way of bigamy. Many in our day choose to have an affair instead. Others just mentally check out of the relationship.

But there is a better way. And that's where I want to spend the bulk of our time in this chapter.

WHAT DO YOU DO WHEN YOU DON'T LOVE THE ONE YOU'RE WITH?

That's the big question. And you need to know, right up front, that I believe that if a Christian husband and wife are both determined to find a way to love each other — that, in fact, God can restore their love! I believe that. I believe it for two reasons:

First, because the Bible commands marital love. And God would never require from us something that we cannot control.

And secondly, because I've seen it happen. I have personally witnessed dozens of couples who, convinced their love was dead, employed these simple principles I am about to give you — and watched a rekindling take place. So if you really would like to see your love rekindled, if you would love to have the warmth return to your home — keep reading. And don't you dare say it's impossible until you give it a try.

Step #1: STOP EXPECTING FROM YOUR MATE WHAT YOU CAN'T GIVE TO YOUR MATE

In a way, I feel sorry for Jacob. I don't think anyone could have fulfilled the expectations he built up over that seven-year period of hard labor! Not even Rachel. Really! I'm convinced that even if he *had* married her first — the morning after the wedding, he probably still would have awakened, thinking, *"That's all there is?"*

We have the same problem. From childhood, we're exposed to wonderful stories about Prince Charming riding in on a white horse and rescuing the fair young princess. He kisses her, they fall in love at first sight, and then ride away into the sunset, to live — are you with me? HAPPILY EVER AFTER! Of course, these stories never mention such mundane realities as a job, children, ex-girlfriends, bills, emotional scars — no! That would be too unromantic! They just lived — happily ever after.

As we grew older, we began to wonder, *"How will I know when I meet my Prince Charming?"* And we were told, *"Don't worry. When you meet him . . . you'll know. God has somebody out there just for you. So keep your eyes peeled, and one of these days you'll meet him — and you'll know."*

And so we spend our late teen years and early adult years looking. Waiting *to know*. Some more obsessed than others. Elizabeth Jolley, in her book, *Cabin Fever,* wrote:

> "I experience again the deep-felt wish to be part of a married couple, to sit by the fire in winter with the man who is my husband. So intense is this wish that if I write the word husband on a piece of paper, my eyes fill with tears."³

And then we make our decision. We stand before the altar and make those ridiculously insane promises. But the trouble is, after an entire lifetime of incredibly unrealistic expectations, we're not really marrying the person — we're marrying our dream.

Herein lies the problem: Nobody can live up to that kind of billing! I love the story of the man who visited prison one day. He and his tour guide approached a man in a padded cell who was beating his head against the wall. He kept saying over and again,

> "*Linda, how could you do it? How could you do it!*"
> His guide said, "*You see, he was in love with Linda, but she jilted him. So he went nuts and here he is!*"
> They went to the next cell, and there was another man also beating his head against the wall, saying, "*Linda, how could you do it?*"
> The man said, "*What's **his** story?*" The guide said, "*Oh, he married Linda!*"

You see, we have too high a view of this thing. We are obsessed with unrealistic expectations. We enter marriage demanding more from a union than any normal human could possibly deliver.

Christian women expect their husbands to be clones of Jesus Himself. Kind and gentle, yet strong and protective. Insightful and wise, yet vulnerable and weak. He should lead his family in prayer and worship, yet also be at the peak of his chosen career.

And we all know what Christian men want. They want her to

be always available and yet also to maintain a career; they want her to take care of the home, the kids and the husband — but still have enough energy to look like Sharon Stone, and be responsive to his advances whenever he takes the notion!

The problem is, marriage simply cannot bear up under the weight of such mythological dreaming! No one could ever fulfill such a kaleidoscope of expectation!

Give it up, friend. There is no such thing as an ideal marriage. There is no such person as an ideal mate. To think such a thing, according to H.L. Mencken, is to abide in a *"state of perpetual anesthesia — to mistake an ordinary young man for a Greek god or an ordinary young woman for a goddess!"* Get real!

And until you do get real, you'll keep believing that if you had just married the right person, you'd feel the way you ought to feel. NO. Even the most complementary-constructed couples have plenty of disappointments. Because there is no way that two imperfect, scarred people could ever come up with a perfect union. The fact is, the only thing perfect about **your** marriage is the God Who joined you together.

Are you with me? You need to stop demanding that your mate be perfect. That he fulfill your every dream, that she meet your every need — and instead, start looking to the only ONE WHO **IS** PERFECT! The only One Who can take your marriage, no matter how imperfect the participants, and make it into a thing of immaculate beauty!

Step #2: STOP ENTERTAINING THOUGHTS OF INVOLVEMENT WITH ANYONE ELSE BUT YOUR MATE

You see, you made a promise on your wedding day. A promise that went something like this:

> *"Steve Wyatt, do you take this woman to be your wedded wife, to live together after God's ordinance in the holy estate of matrimony? Will you love her, comfort her, honor and keep her in sickness and in health and forsaking all others keep*

yourself only to her so long as you both shall live?"

And Steve Wyatt replies: *"I WIIIILLLLL!"*

Why, no wonder moms and dads cry, grandparents bite their lips, bridesmaids' knees shake and the best man's palms sweat! This is major stuff!

George Bernard Shaw wrote:

> *"When two people are under the influence of the most violent, most insane, most delusive, and most transient of passions, they are required to swear that they will remain in that excited, abnormal, and exhausting condition continuously until death do them part."*

And you know? HE'S RIGHT! They say that love is blind. And it is, until after the ceremony. Then it doesn't take long for both parties to sing, *"I was blind . . . but now I clearly see!"* And he realizes she's not a fairy princess after all. In fact, she's terrifyingly similar to his mother-in-law! And she discovers that he's no Prince Charming either. Why, he's got some ugly habits that drive her up a wall! And they both discover, doggone it, that there are a lot of good-looking women and kind, compassionate men out there! *And I don't know how it happened, preacher, but I have strong feelings for someone other than my mate!*

Now our culture lies to us at this very moment. Because culture says:

> *If you have those feelings, you must act on them. Because those feelings are strong evidence that your marriage is wrong for you — and this other person will be for you what your mate could never be!*

Friend, that's a lie. Now you won't hear that in very many places in this culture — perhaps in no other place than among the household of faith, but if you direct your energies and your emotions toward anyone other than your mate, you will reap horrendous destruction. Because you're married, friend. And if you're married, you are at the point in life when it is no longer what you want to do or what you feel like doing that matters.

What matters is — YOU MADE A VOW TO GOD! And you'd better keep it!

Winston Churchill was right: *Wars are not won by evacuation.* And your marriage will never be restored if you bail out. So stop entertaining thoughts of external involvement.

Third, if you would rekindle your love, you must also start some things. For one, you must:

Step #3: START PRAYING FOR GOD'S POWER TO CHANGE THE WAY YOU FEEL

Do you have an alien affection? The first thing you must start is PRAYING. You need to pray that God will remove that wrongful desire.

We Christians say with our lips that God can do anything; but when it comes to our marriage we like to hedge our bets. *God, I know you can part the Red Sea; I know You can rescue Daniel from the lion's mouth, I know you can walk on water, and even raise the dead; but the one thing I don't think you can do is restore my love for my spouse."*

Now you wouldn't dream of saying that; but that's the way many feel. And that's basically what you're saying to God when you claim that the feelings are gone and instead of trusting His power to change those feelings — you just *"throw in the towel."* In a sense, every divorce is an admission on the part of one or both that there was something in that marriage that was too hard for God.

And yet Scripture clearly says, **"I am the LORD, the God of all mankind. Is anything too hard for me?"** (Jer 32:27). Scripture replies: **"For nothing is impossible with God"** (Luke 1:37).

You say you have no love for your spouse? You say the feelings are gone? Well, before you pack your bags, hit your knees. And pray that God will change your heart. Don't ask God to change your mate — ask Him to change you. To restore to *you*

His healing power of abiding, steadfast love. He is able, so just ask.

Are you with me? Pray, but don't stop after the prayer. You need to also take step #4:

Step #4: START ACTING *TOWARD* YOUR MATE THE WAY YOU WISH YOU FELT *ABOUT* YOUR MATE

Now admittedly, this is the toughest step to take. It's the step Jacob refused to take. Instead of actively choosing to love Leah, he passively allowed the jealousies and insecurities to rage — bouncing from tent to tent — procreating with whomever he was with — which only served to make matters worse! *Evidently, he wanted to feel the right thing before he did the right thing.* DOES THAT SOUND FAMILIAR?

But you know what I've discovered? You won't feel it until you do it. I came across a true account from the life of Dr. George Crane, a psychologist and nationally syndicated columnist. A woman came to him and said she wanted to divorce her husband. But she didn't want to just get out of the marriage — she wanted to get even. She was ticked at this man! She asked Dr. Crane to help her. He said,

> *"I'll help you get even. If you really want to get even with him, here's what you do. Go back home and act as if you really love him. Tell him how much he means to you. Praise all of his good qualities. Mention every decent trait. Go out of your way to be kind. Fix his favorite meal. Be generous to him. Do whatever you can to convince him of your eternal, undying love. Then, when you have him convinced — DUMP HIM!"*

She said, *"That's a great idea!"*

And she went home and did everything just as she was told. Anything that she thought might convince him that she really loved him, she did. She didn't show for the next appointment, so Crane called and said,

Behind the Tent Flaps

"Are you ready now to go through with your divorce?"

She said, *"Divorce? Never! I found out that I really love the guy!"*

Of course. BECAUSE SHE ACTED! You see, it's my conviction that if you do acts of love even when you don't feel the love, that the feelings will return. Eventually the cycle will complete itself. However, if you wait for the feelings to return before you do anything, you'll *never* do anything — and the relationship will die.

Now I'm not smart enough to come up with that on my own. C.S. Lewis said it before me. He was once asked, *"How do you love a neighbor when you don't love your neighbor?"* He replied, *"Act as if you do."*

Marilyn vos Savant, listed in the *Guinness Book of World Records* under "Highest IQ," was asked, *"What do you do when your emotions are at war with your intellect?"* She replied,

> *"When there's a conflict, I find that if I act on my intellect, my emotions will follow. With most things in life, what IS good eventually will FEEL good, but what merely FEELS good eventually feels bad."*

WOW! That's great stuff, isn't it?

So whether you feel it or not — if you're married, you've made a commitment. And having prayed for your heart to change, you need to get up off your knees and do something about it. Now maybe you can't take huge, giant steps, but you can take a few baby steps. Here are some suggestions that might help you get started:

> Be interested in her friends.
> Ask her opinion.
> Value her suggestions.
> Respect his decisions.
> Comfort her when she is down.
> Learn to enjoy football.
> > Or basketball.
> > Or underwater basket weaving.

Compliment her often.
Show her you need her.
Admit your mistakes.
Write him a letter.
Surprise her with flowers.
Get rid of habits that annoy her.
Hold her hand in public.
Suggest physical contact instead of waiting for him.
Learn to enjoy shopping.
Call her when you're going to be late.

The point is — act the way you wish you felt. *Because it's far easier to act yourself into the right way of feeling than it is to feel yourself into the right way of acting.*

Now when you start doing that — when you start acting in a loving way toward your mate — you must decide to ignore whether your mate decides to start meeting your needs or not. Marital love is not a matter of *"if I scratch your back, you're gonna scratch mine,"* right? No. True love does what is right even if there is no return on the investment.

I love the story of the young medical student who was out on a date and began whispering sweet nothings into his lovely date's ear. She was kind-of impressed, but never went out with him again. *Why?* Because she realized later that all of the time he was saying those wonderful things to her — he had his finger on her pulse so he could see how she was responding.

Forget how he's coming along. Ignore her progress. Remember that it is your responsibility to love your mate; it's God's responsibility to change him. Or her. So . . . start meeting your mate's needs instead of focusing on your own needs.

Then finally:

Step #5: START VIEWING YOUR MARRIAGE AS PERMANENT, AND RELEASE ALL PLANS FOR DEPARTURE

I love the comment by Ruth Graham, wife of evangelist Billy

Behind the Tent Flaps

Graham. A reporter asked the couple if they had ever considered divorce. Their immediate response was, "NO!" But Mrs. Graham had more to say. *"Divorce? NO. But murder? Sometimes!"* You see, even the best of relationships will have struggles. There will be times when you will feel used. Put down. Taken for granted. There will be moments when your partner may not actually deserve your love. There will be times when you won't feel what you know you ought to feel. It is in those moments that true love says,

"I will stand by you. I will love you anyway. My love to you is permanent. It's not 'I love you until, or as long as, or if...' it's forever. I am your man now and I will always be your man."

Any other kind of love is without effect. And only when I know that the love you have for me is a permanent deal — will I give up my securities, my masks, my roles, and my games. I will not open myself to a temporary, tentative love, to an offer which has a lot of fine print and far too many footnotes in the contract.

That's the way Jill Williams felt. Even though Pat had begun his long and arduous attempt to restore her love for him — a journey that he has recorded in a fine book entitled, *Rekindled* (a book you ought to read, one that echoes many of the things I've written in this chapter), it took a long time before Jill was willing to believe that his attempts were genuine, that the change was permanent. But finally, the same woman who said, *"I would rather be any place in the world than here..."* — that same woman wrote a note and addressed it to *"the greatest husband in the world."* It read as follows:

Dear Pat,
  I love you so much for your response to that darkest hour two years ago today. That you would share your name, life, love, and yourself with me is truly my dream come true. There aren't enough words to express my love and devotion to you. I am the most blessed of all women.
  Love,
  Jill[4]

Yes, your love can be rekindled. No, not apart from your effort. And no, not apart from God's power. But if you will surrender your will to His plan, He can help rekindle the love you think is dead. He did it for Pat and Jill. He did it for Isaac and Rebekah. He could have done it for Jacob and Leah.

And whether He does it for you and your mate — is entirely up to you.

NOTES

[1] Copyright 1949, 1973 by Richard Rodgers and Oscar Hammerstein 2nd (New York: Williamson Music, Inc.)

[2] From *Fiddler on the Roof,* by Joseph Stein, Jerry Bock and Sheldon Harnick. Copyright 1964 by Joseph Stein. Music and lyrics Copyright 1964 by Sunbeam Music Corp. Permission to reprint any portions of the play must be obtained from the publisher: Crown Publishers, Inc., 419 Park Avenue South, New York, N.Y. 10016.

[3] Elizabeth Jolley, *Cabin Fever* (New York: Harper Perennial, 1990).

[4] Pat and Jill Williams, *Rekindled* (Old Tappan: Revell, 1985).

CHAPTER TWO

Wounds from Sticks and Stones Heal Better

GENESIS 12:10-20

On August 12, 1961, under cover of night, the East German government erected a wall. An infamous wall. A wall of division. A wall topped with barbed wire, intending to separate east from west, dividing a city and a nation asunder. The Berlin Wall was built despite fierce international cries of protest. Tensions between East and West were running strong in those days. And yet, not long after it was built, President John F. Kennedy stood just a few feet from that wall and delivered a moving address. As he concluded his remarks, the President attempted to diffuse some of the tension, by speaking this phrase: *"Ich bin ein Berliner."* Strictly translated, the phrase was a point of identification. Taken literally, the President had said, *"I am a Berliner."* However, according to *Newsweek Magazine,* in the common vernacular of the people, what he *really* said was, *"I am a jelly doughnut."*

Which reminds me of a greeting card I saw sometime ago. It read:

*"I know you think you understand what you thought I said,
but I'm not sure that what you thought you heard
is what I meant to say."*

Isn't that real? We say things we don't mean, and often we mean the things we never say — and unfortunately, no matter how hard we try — honest, forthright, accurate communication takes it on the chin.

Even in the best of times — communication is an uphill climb. **Especially is that true in marriage.** Zeke and May had been married for over seventy years. Zeke was 101 years old, and May was 99. One hot afternoon they sat on the front porch rocking. The old man was nearly deaf. His wife looked at him with admiration in her eyes and said, *"Zeke, I'm proud of you."* He looked around and said, *"What's that you say, May?"* She raised her voice, *"I'm proud of you!"* He looked away, and then replied, *"I'm tired of you, too, May."*

Now if communication is dicey even when times are good — then communication is a real gamble when times are bad — *when conflict is injected into the relationship.*

And don't try to tell me that you don't have any conflict. Any couple who tells you that they never argue, that they never exchange cross words — why, they'll lie to you about other things, too.

Ed Young tells the story of the time he ministered a church in Canton, North Carolina. He had just voiced a similar sentiment, and following the service, a woman walked out with husband in tow, and headed right for Ed. She was a "pit bull" of a woman, and her eyes blazed as she said, *"Preacher, you have told something that is not true today. We've been married forty-eight years and we stand here as a testimony. We have never had a cross word in all our years of marriage. Isn't that right, L.L.?"* Knowing his cue, L.L. replied, *"That's right, preacher, never a cross word."* Ed writes:

> "Those initials, by the way, stood for 'Little Love.' And quite literally, that was what he had known in his 48-year marriage: little love and almost total domination. And I still believe that any couple who says they have never argued is either lying or one partner is totally dominating the other."[1]

He's right. And the question before the house is, *How do you handle it when those conflicts come? It's inevitable that they will happen, so what do you do when they arrive?*

Wounds from Sticks and Stones Heal Better

Some years ago, a story appeared on the wires of the United Press International. It said that a young New York bride had gotten into an argument with her husband — just a few hours after their wedding — and she had run him over with the family car, killing him. The county district attorney said that the twenty-one year old bride drove over her twenty-three year old husband because the couple had experienced a strong disagreement over an incident that had occurred at their reception.

That's one way to handle marital conflict. And quite a permanent solution, I might add. Others, however, opting for a less dramatic display, respond by exploding into a raving tantrum. They throw things, they curse, and some even hit their spouses. Still others respond with tears. Now tears can be healthy, but they can also be used to stifle communication. To manipulate the perceived aggressor into backing down.

Another response is the silent treatment. This is an especially favorite tool among Christians. Because Christians, after all, aren't supposed to *get* angry — and since we want to appear mature and in control — we just pout. We punish our mate with silence.

"Is there something wrong, honey?"
"No."
"Are you sure?"
"Yes."
"Do you want to talk?"
"No."

And the resulting silence is deafening. The hostilities continue to fester, and the perceived offender has no idea what in the world he has done. And until he figures it out, the boycott won't be lifted.

Some mates respond to conflict with judgmental attitudes. Or by bringing up past iniquities. One man said, *"Every time my wife and I get into a conflict, she gets historical."*

A friend asked, "You mean hysterical?"

"No," he said, *"Historical! She brings up everything wrong I've ever done!"*

Some deal with conflict by dodging the confrontation. Some enjoy overstating the issue, or overdramatizing the problem. Still others love to butt in and interrupt their accuser. Yet others view the whole scene as a game — where someone wins and someone else (preferably the other guy) loses.

ABRAHAM AND SARAH: HOW NOT TO HANDLE CONFLICT

Now what you may not realize is that such tactics are not new. In fact, they are as old as Scripture itself. In this chapter, I want to pull back the tent flaps and show you how one of the greatest couples in Scripture handled their conflict. *And to be honest, there was a time in their marriage when it wasn't a pretty picture.* Despite the fact that Abraham is called **"God's friend"** (James 2:23), and despite the fact that Sarah is held up to all believing women as a model for **"doing what is right"** (1 Pet 3:6), the truth is — they both did an awful lot wrong. *Especially in the realm of communicating in the midst of conflict.*

THE EARLY YEARS

At first, things went pretty well. You may remember that Abraham was quite a wealthy man. He and Sarah had made a good life for themselves in a place that was considered the progressive, elite, paragon of success. They lived in Ur — the choicest city in the region. THE place to live in that day. Anybody who was anybody lived in Ur. Which reminds me of the sign that used to appear at the city limits where I live. It read:

Move To Newburgh And Be Somebody!

Gag! That same civic pride was felt among the Ur-ites. And yet:

> **"The Lord had said to Abram, 'Leave your country, your people and your father's household and go to the land I will show you'"** (Gen 12:1).

Now it's never easy to move, but this was really a toughie! Abraham was an old man! He was 75 years old when he got this command. On top of that he had to consider all of the possessions and livestock that he owned — and they didn't have U-Hauls back then! But the toughest part of all was not knowing where he was to go. Hebrews 11:8 says, **"By faith Abraham, when called to go to a place he would later receive as his inheritance, obeyed and went, *even though he did not know where he was going*"** (emphasis added).

How did Sarah respond to this move? All we're told is:

> "He took his wife Sarai . . . all the possessions they had accumulated . . . and they set out for the land of Canaan" (Gen 12:5).

Knowing Sarah like I do — and you'll know her better as this chapter progresses — I'm quite certain she didn't just roll on this decision. First Peter 3:6 doesn't mean she obeyed without question or without understanding. I'm convinced she had plenty of input. Really! She was a strong-willed, opinionated woman!

Evidently, the two had developed such an intimate relationship with each other and with their God — that despite the fact that the initial reaction must have been shock, and most certainly generated at least a measure of conflict — as they discussed it together, they just knew it was the thing to do!

However it played out, I'll tell you one way it DIDN'T play out:

> *"Honey, we're going to move."*
> "Where?"
> *"I don't know."*
> "Oh. OK!"

Uh-huh. Ain't no way. UNLESS . . . Abraham, being so convinced that God was in this thing, so thoughtfully and carefully communicated his conviction to Sarah, that Sarah, having carefully examined Abraham's heart — could wholeheartedly agree and, in fact, start packing boxes.

THE MIDDLE YEARS

So much for the good times. Hard to believe, but practically overnight, it seems, things got bad. Primarily because, although in the previous verses, we found Abraham trusting God for a major move to a location he knew not where — all of a sudden . . . Abraham starts doing his own thing.

> "Now there was a famine in the land, and Abram went down to Egypt to live there for a while because the famine was severe" (Gen 12:10).

Without in any measure discounting the fear associated with famines — a careful reading of verse 10 reveals that Abraham had made a serious error in judgment. Read that verse again. It doesn't say that God told him to go to Egypt. It doesn't say that Abraham prayed about it or that he even sought the mind of God. And even though in the previous nine verses Abraham refused to make a move unless God was in it — suddenly, he panics and heads for Egypt.

> "As he was about to enter Egypt, he said to his wife Sarai, 'I know what a beautiful woman you are'" (Gen 12:11).

Now isn't that a nice compliment? And wives love to hear such things from their husbands — but after a few years of marriage, far too often a compliment like that is followed by a request like this:

> "'When the Egyptians see you, they will say, 'This is his wife.' Then they will kill me but will let you live. Say you are my sister, so that I will be treated well for your sake and my life will be spared because of you'" (Gen 12:12-13).

DON'T WORRY HONEY, I'VE GOT A PLAN!

Now in a very strict sense, Abraham wasn't asking her to lie. The fact is, Abraham and Sarah had the same father; they just had different mothers. So it's kind of a half-truth that Abraham was asking. He also clearly understood the marriage laws of Egypt. In Egypt, if you wanted to marry someone, you had to negotiate the price with the bride's family. And he thought, *"If someone wants Sarah, I'll just set the price so high no one would dare pay it! And in that way, she'll be protected, and so will I."*

But the problem with this plan is that the one he's most interested in protecting is himself. Starting with the little jaunt to Egypt, and now this carnal plan of deception, Abraham has clearly begun to live life on his terms. So he says to his wife,

"You're a good-looking woman! And I know these people. When they see someone your age in as good a shape as you are in — they're going to want you! So just tell them you're my sister. Don't worry, I'll bargain you out of any trouble — but just play along, or they might kill me!"

Keil and Delitzch are two Old Testament commentators not typically known for humor. In fact, their work, although considered quite definitive — is also quite dry. But here's what they have to say about Abraham's scheme:

"As Sarah was then 65 years old, her beauty at such an age, has been made a difficulty by some. But as she lived to the age of 127, she was then middle-aged. And as her vigor and bloom had not been tried by bearing children, she might easily appear very beautiful in the eyes of the Egyptians, whose wives, according to both ancient and modern testimony, were generally ugly and faded early."[2]

Isn't that great? And sure enough:

"When Abram came to Egypt, the Egyptians saw that she was a very beautiful woman. And when Pharaoh's officials saw her, they praised her to Pharaoh, and she was taken into his palace" (Gen 12:14-15).

You see, Pharaoh was exempt from the laws of negotiation. If he wanted someone, he got her. And just like that — Sarah is hustled into Pharaoh's harem! ABRAHAM'S PLAN HAS GONE BUST! If he says anything now, he'll be killed for sure. If he says nothing, Sarah will be violated by a pagan. Verse 16 says that Pharaoh . . .

". . . treated Abram well for her sake, and Abram acquired sheep and cattle, male and female donkeys, menservants and maidservants, and camels" (Gen 12:16).

Which is yet another reminder that you cannot view external prosperity as a sign of God's approval on your life. Abraham has just compromised his wife into sin, and yet he starts getting all this neat, new stuff! And it would be easy for Abraham to think, because of this unexpected windfall, his plan was obviously God's will. *It was not.*

> "But the LORD inflicted serious diseases on Pharaoh and his household because of Abram's wife Sarai" (Gen 12:17).

If Abraham isn't going to care for his wife, God will.

> "So Pharaoh summoned Abram. 'What have you done to me?' he said. 'Why didn't you tell me she was your wife? Why did you say, 'She is my sister,' so that I took her to be my wife? Now then, here is your wife. Take her and go!'" (Gen 12:18-19).

How far Abraham had fallen! He had been a believer! He once was one who walked by faith. But now? This man of faith, this **"friend of God"** is being rebuked by a godless heathen! A crocodile-hugging, frog-kissing, beetle-worshiping pagan!

And with that, the downward cycle begins.

As we turn our attention to Genesis 16, we're reminded that, along with the command to move, God also gave Abraham a promise. He had said to him, *"You are going to have family that cannot be numbered. It will be like the sands of the seashore and the stars in the heavens."* And yet several years pass — and there's no baby. No child. Not even a failed pregnancy. Nothing! Now Abraham was no spring chicken. He was 75 when God gave him this promise. And by the time we come to chapter 16, he's in his mid-80's, and has begun to panic. So has Sarah. She fears that her biological clock has stopped ticking — that there's no way God can fulfill His promise! Here are the facts:

> "Now Sarai, Abram's wife, had borne him no children. But she had an Egyptian maidservant named Hagar" (Gen 16:1).

You can almost read her mind, can't you? Frustrated by God's delay, Sarah starts looking at this thing from the human viewpoint. *But don't you dare criticize her, because you and I do the same thing.* In the midst of some marital conflict (and if you've never faced the prospect of a barren womb, you don't know the kind of conflict it can bring) or in the face of some insurmountable problem — especially when you're tired of waiting for God to intervene — why, everyone has known the temptation to rush in and fix it. So don't you judge her. Just see that, although Sarah had been brutally victimized because her husband had failed to trust God —because he tried to handle it on his own — she falls prey to the exact same temptation. She comes to Abraham and says,

> "'The LORD has kept me from having children. Go, sleep with my maidservant; perhaps I can build a family through her.' Abram agreed to what Sarai said" (Gen 16:2).

You thought surrogate mothers was a nineties kind of thing? Think again. It goes all the way back to Genesis! Primarily because Abraham passively listened to his wife's fleshly plan.

It's at this point that some husbands would like me to stop and make application. They want me to say something stupid like, *"And here is biblical evidence that you should never listen to your wife."* Think again, guys! If I were stupid enough to say that, I wouldn't have anywhere to go tonight. And I like where I live! Besides, it would be a self-serving diatribe, not to mention a very foolish, wholly inaccurate application. Truth is, some of the best counsel I have ever received was from my wife.

But just like Abraham had stumbled, so also Sarah. She fell prey to the temptation toward human engineering. And Abraham, just like so many passive males today — sat there like an idiot and nodded his head.

> **"He slept with Hagar, and she conceived."** [And that's when the trouble started. Because as soon as . . .] **"she knew she was pregnant, she began to despise her mistress"** (Gen 16:4).

In other words, she rubbed Sarah's nose in it. *I gave your husband a baby, and you didn't.* And suddenly, this plan that had once seemed to so very right — now had gone so very wrong!

> **"Then Sarai said to Abram, 'You are responsible for the wrong I am suffering. I put my servant in your arms, and now that she knows she is pregnant, she despises me. May the LORD judge between you and me'"** (Gen 16:5).

Behind the Tent Flaps

TIME OUT! Without taking away in any sense the fact that Abraham made his choice and, without a whole lot of convincing, headed for Hagar's tent — not letting him off the hook at all, the fact is, IT WAS SARAH'S IDEA! She made the suggestion, he just did the follow-through. Yet as soon as Sarah's plan hits muddy water — she cries foul!

HOW COULD YOU DO SUCH A THING?

I came across the story of a manager of a minor league baseball team who was so disgusted with his center fielder's performance that he ordered him into the dugout and assumed the position himself. The first ball that came into center field took a bad hop and hit the manager in the mouth. The next one was a high fly ball that got lost in the glare of the sun, and it bounced off of his forehead. The third was a hard line drive that he charged with outstretched arms, but it slipped through his glove and smashed his nose. Furious, he ran back to the dugout, grabbed the center fielder by his jersey and shouted, *"You idiot! You've got center field so messed up, I can't do a thing with it!"*

Blame. How quickly we dish it out. How slowly we receive it from others. We're like the third grader who said to his teacher, *"Miss Smith, I don't want to scare you, but my dad said if my grades don't improve, somebody's gonna get a spanking."*

Blame. It's the oldest trick in the book. It goes all the way back to Adam and Eve. Adam, after having received clear instruction not to eat the fruit, ate it anyway. When confronted by God, rather than accept responsibility for his sin, Adam fingered Eve saying, **"It's her fault!"** What did Eve do? She fingered the serpent and said, **"It's the snake's fault!"**

And ever since, the story line has remained the same.

"It's your fault."
"It's not my fault. It was your idea."
"It may have been my idea, but you're the one who did it!"

When will we learn that blame never heals? It always hurts. That blame never makes people whole in their relationships; it only breaks relationships? That blame never unites; it only divides? That blame never builds; it only tears down? That blame never solves a problem; it only compounds the problem?

I tell you, Abraham is between the proverbial rock and the hard place. *Don't you find yourself feeling for this guy?*

"*I thought I did what you wanted!*"

"I didn't want it to turn out like this!"

"*But you told me . . .*"

"Don't tell me what I told you — HOW COULD YOU DO SUCH A THING?"

"*But you said . . .*"

"Don't you quote me! You're the one!"

No wonder Abraham sighed and said:

> **"'Your servant is in your hands,' Abram said. 'Do with her whatever you think best.' Then Sarai mistreated Hagar; so she fled from her"** (Gen 16:6).

I'm waving the white flag. I'm giving up. Do what you want to do. And as a result, do you know who got the shaft in this deal? **HAGAR.** And Hagar's son. Who was also Abraham's son.

You see, some husbands respond to conflict just like Abraham. Wanting peace at any price, tired of rocking the boat, hoping to avoid any future hassle — he becomes a weenie. A passive, uninvolved, disconnected non-entity.

If there's one common strain I hear from wives, it's this: *Steve, my husband turns off when he comes home. He's such a great success in his career, and I know he's really making things happen down at the office — but in the home? He's here, but he's not here!*

Remember the movie, *Dances With Wolves?* Kevin Costner was named by the Indians according to his most prominent trait. A lot of wives seem to think that their husbands ought to be renamed, too. "*Sits with paper.*" Or, "*Sleeps on couch.*" Or, "*Watches the game.*"

Listen, guys, don't check out of your relationship. You may think that non-involvement is the only pathway to peace. I'm telling you, there's no peace on that path at all. As we'll see a bit later, Abraham paid a heavy price for his passivity.

Let's move on to Genesis 18. Abraham and Sarah are still waiting for that promised baby. They have just received new assurances that God was still in this thing. And yet the facts hadn't changed:

> **"Abraham and Sarah were already old and well advanced in years, and Sarah was past the age of childbearing. So Sarah laughed to herself as she thought, 'After I am worn out and my master is old, will I now have this pleasure?"** (Gen 18:11-12).

Guess who was eavesdropping when she made that comment? That's right — the Lord. He said to Abraham . . .

> **"'Why did Sarah laugh and say, 'Will I really have a child, now that I am old?' Is anything too hard for the LORD? I will return to you at the appointed time next year and Sarah will have a son.' Sarah was afraid, so she lied and said, 'I did not laugh. 'But he said, 'yes, you did laugh'"** (Gen 18:13-15).

Isn't that real?

Did not.
Did too.
Did not.
Lord, I didn't mean it the way you took it.
"You did, too. Sarah, don't lie; you've given up and you know it. That's why you laughed!"

What she was really saying was: "THINGS WILL NEVER CHANGE. *This is the way it's gonna be; I guess I'm just gonna have to live with it!"*

Is that how you approach marital conflict? **"Steve, I'd *like* to put my marriage back together, but I don't think he can change!"** Or as in one case I remember, **"Steve, he HAS changed, but I'm not convinced that it's real!"** *Do you know what are you saying when you say that?* You're saying that the way things HAVE been are the way they will ALWAYS be, so let's stop kidding ourselves. A leopard can't change his spots and my husband isn't going to change his ways either.

And yet the stuff that true, marital love is made of, is abiding, sustaining hope. Hope that believes that that ornery husband of yours really *can* change. That that disinterested wife really *can* have a change of heart. Someone has said that there is no such thing as a *"hopeless situation; only people who have grown hopeless about their situation."* Isn't that true? Yet far too often, when someone with whom we have a relationship gets messed up — we write 'em off! And in so doing, we fulfill our own prophecy: *"Aw, he'll never change."*

Whenever I hear that, I usually agree. Then I say, *"As long as that's the way you feel — you're right! He won't change."* Because there's no hope to drive him, no faith to sustain him! But true love, godly love, is *always* hopeful, *always* trusting, *always* believing for your mate possibilities for change.

You may find this hard to believe — but do you remember Abraham's blunder back in Egypt? Remember when he tried to pass his wife off as his sister? Well, believe it or not — he did it again. Now don't too get prideful about that; something tells me you have a familiar sin, too. Am I right? Some secret sin that you keep confessing over and over and over again? Instead of judging Abraham, maybe you ought to just thank God He's not writing Scripture anymore!

It's a different location, but beyond that, it's the same scene.

> **"Now Abraham moved on from there into the region of the Negev and lived between Kadesh and Shur. For a while he stayed in Gerar"** (Gen 20:1).

Who knows why he went to Gerar? One thing's for sure: There is no indication in Scripture that God told him to go.

> **"And there Abraham said of his wife Sarah, 'She is my sister.' Then Abimelech king of Gerar sent for Sarah and took her"** (Gen 20:2).

Because she was a good looking woman! And, as far as he knew, she was available! Once again, Abraham is taking care of #1. Which left God to have to protect #2. And sure enough . . .

> **"God came to Abimelech in a dream one night and said to him, 'You are as good as dead because of the woman you**

have taken; she is a married woman.' Now Abimelech had not gone near her, so he said, 'LORD, will you destroy an innocent nation? Did he not say to me, 'She is my sister,' and didn't she also say, 'He is my brother'? I have done this with a clear conscience and clean hands'" (Gen 20:3-5).

Can you believe that? A believer lies and puts not only his wife, but also an unbeliever in moral jeopardy! The sad thing is, Abraham should never have panicked. Didn't God say that he and Sarah were going to have a son? And as long as they were still childless — doesn't it make sense to believe that there was no way any king was going to kill him? He had to father a son! You don't father sons if you're a corpse. But Abraham forgot that little tidbit, and as a result, Abimelech was in deep weeds.

> "Then God said to him in the dream, 'Yes, I know you did this with a clear conscience, and so I have kept you from sinning against me. That is why I did not let you touch her. Now return the man's wife, for he is a prophet, and he will pray for you and you will live. But if you do not return her, you may be sure that you and all yours will die.' Early the next morning Abimelech summoned all his officials, and when he told them all that had happened, they were very much afraid. Then Abimelech called Abraham in and said, 'What have you done to us? How have I wronged you that you have brought such great guilt upon me and my kingdom? You have done things to me that should not be done.' And Abimelech asked Abraham, 'What was your reason for doing this?'" (Gen 20:6-10).

What possessed you, man? Isn't it a sad commentary when even the pagans can indict the believers? Abimelech was a man of integrity, and he points the finger at a professing believer who was living a lie.

Do you know how Abraham responded? Did he say, *"I'm sorry. I guess I really blew my testimony, didn't I?"* NO. Instead, he claimed: ***"I DIDN'T DO ANYTHING WRONG!"*** Do you see it in verse 11?

> "Abraham replied, 'I said to myself, 'There is surely no fear of God in this place, and they will kill me because of my wife'" (Gen 20:11).

In other words, *I did it because you people don't fear God.* That's why I lied. And yet the truth is, the very thing he saw as absent in Abimelech was exactly what was missing in his life, too. Abraham feared Abimelech more than God. And so he compromised.

He also said: *"Besides, I didn't really lie."*

"She really is my sister, the daughter of my father though not of my mother; and she became my wife" (Gen 20:12).

Then he adds:

"And when God had me wander from my father's household, I said to her, 'This is how you can show your love to me: Everywhere we go, say of me, 'He is my brother'" (Gen 20:13).

Look at the first phrase: **"And when God had me wander..."** Which translated means, *"It's God's fault. If He had just let me stay in Ur, none of this would have happened!"*

Now we're not told this in the text, but I imagine Sarah, watching Abraham from the sidelines, listening to her man cowardly rejecting any and all responsibility for his actions — and having herself been put (once again) in a perilous position of sexual and emotional jeopardy, having been placed in a position of vulnerability by a husband who cared more for his own protection than for hers — I'm convinced she could have spit! It's true, you know. Whenever you're forced to watch your mate scramble for his reputation, whenever you have to witness his frantic attempts to explain his own reprehensible behavior — it takes a toll.

Besides, she was beginning to feel the sting of a little phrase that men still use today to get what they want from their *woman*. Did you catch it there in verse 13?

"'This is how you can show your love to me...'" (Gen 20:13b).

Ladies, have you ever heard that line before? "If you really love me..." Sure you have. And girls? Any time you hear that line? RUN! It's a red flag if there's ever been a red flag! These are the favorite words of the abuser! *Come here, honey. You love daddy, don't you?* Or, *If you really loved me, you'd watch this porn . . . you'd let me have this affair . . . you'd do whatever perversion I want you to do — if you really loved me!*

Now if theirs had been a healthy relationship — if these two had cultivated an atmosphere of honesty and strength — Sarah might have said, *"No way, José! Loving you is not the issue. The issue is — this is wrong! Supporting you is one thing. Lying for you is another. Being your mate is a joy, being your patsy is a pain."* The trouble is, Abraham and Sarah's marriage had become so enshrouded with half-truths and veiled threats and empty promises — that honest, open communication had been absent for a long, long time!

And that's why it was inevitable that things would eventually come to a head. And boy did they ever! In Genesis 21, the big day has finally arrived! This 100-year old man and his 90-year old bride have just birthed a brand-new baby boy! And they're so thrilled, they name him *Laughter!* Isaac. And suddenly, they have a new lease on life! The trouble is, the old lease hadn't run out.

I'm referring to **Ishmael.** Abraham's son through the servant Hagar. By God's direction, they had returned to Abraham and Sarah, and Ishmael, by this time, is now a big, strapping teenager — while Isaac is just a little squirt.

"The child grew and was weaned, and on the day Isaac was weaned Abraham held a great feast. But Sarah saw that the son whom Hagar the Egyptian had borne to Abraham was mocking . . ." (Gen 20:8-9).

Mocking who? Isaac, that's who. Ishmael was pestering his little brother, as older brothers are known to do. Ishmael was aggravating his kid stepbrother. But Sarah didn't take kindly to this half-breed messing with her baby. So she said . . .

"'Get rid of that slave woman and her son!'" (Gen 20:10a).

Can't you just feel the reverberations? *Get that kid out of my face!*

Now understand, as with most marital conflicts, the hostility was not so much prompted by Ishmael's teasing as it was the whole history of the last several years of their lives that came crashing in. Kids will be kids — but Sarah's feeling the pinch of guilt. She's angry at herself, at Abraham, and even at God. And her contrived solution to the pain? *Get rid of Hagar!*

Then she adds:

> **"'For that slave woman's son will never share in the inheritance with my son Isaac'"** (Gen 20:10b).

You who are in blended families have no doubt heard that line. But wait a minute: He's not just the slave woman's son, he's Abraham's son too! *I don't care! If you want this marriage to survive, get her out of here!*

MAY I POINT OUT THREE MISTAKES SARAH MADE IN THIS CONFRONTATION?

First, it wasn't the right place. Understanding that she was hurt, that she had a legitimate complaint to lodge — the fact is, Abraham was throwing a feast! It was a party! It was a great moment in Abraham's life — and right in front of his nearest and dearest friends, she lets him have it!

Don't ever do that. Marital conflict deserves to be hashed out in privacy. And when you take a swing at your mate in public — whether in the hallways of your church or as a veiled prayer request in your small group — it reveals to all who understand that yours is a bitter, angry, wrathful heart. That you have been seized by rage.

Don't air your dirty laundry. There are places where issues can and should be addressed. But no matter how bad it feels, don't duke it out in public.

Now if it wasn't the right place, ***it obviously wasn't the right time, either.*** Which reminds me of a comment Henry Ward Beecher once made:

> *"Speak when you are angry and you'll make the best speech you will ever regret."*

Timing is everything in marital conflict. One of the reasons this was such a major blow-up is because Abraham and Sarah refused to abide by the words of **Ephesians 4:26: "Do not let the sun go down on your anger, and do not give the devil an opportunity."** These two didn't do that. Instead, they allowed their mutual resentment to build day after day, year after year, decade upon decade! No wonder there was a blow-up! MANY suns had set on their anger!

And then, predictably, she picks the worst possible moment to talk about it! Just as many couples today wait until bedtime. Or the moment hubby comes home from work. Or when mom's facing a mound of dishes and piles of homework and three more loads of laundry!

Wise is the couple who agrees together that the time is right for serious issues. Wise is the husband who realizes that a backyard swim party is not the time to notice that "the Mrs." has "put on a few." Just after Jay Leno's monologue is not a good time to try to make some headway in the area of your family finances or even your sex life.

Do you know what it takes for a 140-pound shortstop to hit a smoking fast ball over a 400-foot fence? TIMING. And if spouses are going to be home-run hitters in marital communication, they, too, will have to develop a sense of timing.

Solomon was right: **"Like apples of gold in settings of silver is a word spoken in right circumstances"** (Prov 25:11, NASB).

And then third, *it wasn't the right spirit, either.*

"The matter distressed Abraham greatly because it concerned his son" (Gen 21:11).

Note that. It *greatly* distressed him. Now maybe Sarah was right. Maybe Hagar and Ishmael did need to move on. But the way she handled it? That wasn't right at all. Scripture admonishes: **"Be angry, and yet do not sin"** (Eph 4:26). That she was angry is understandable. That she allowed her anger to devastate her mate was a sin. Listen, believer, there is no excuse for your lavish displays of temper. There is no justification for your profane tirades. You have no grounds for your hurtful slander and heaping abuse. It's a sin.

THE LATER YEARS

Well, as bad as it got for these two — and it got pretty bad — there was still time for God to work a miracle. And He did. We don't know many of the details, but what we do know is the later years of their lives were marked by a wonderfully gracious and mutual respect and love. *What were the lessons they learned in order for that to happen?* I want to suggest three.

For one, Abraham learned that if your communication with God is on the fritz, your communication at home will be just as troubled.

I find it intriguing that as soon as Abraham stopped listening for God's voice, he also stopped responding to Sarah's need.

So what was it that turned him around? What event could possibly have happened to so thoroughly grab Abraham's attention and turn his heart back toward God and Sarah and others — instead of just on himself? I want to suggest that this life-changing event is the one described in Genesis 22, when God told Abraham to sacrifice his son. To take the fruit of his loins and kill him. And when Abraham raised the blade, ready once again to do as he had done a long time ago — ready to hear God and do His will — he passed the test. You see, it was there on Mt. Moriah that Abraham learned to value the needs of those he loved more than he valued his own needs. It was with hands wrapped tightly about that knife that he learned to trust in God to protect his family and not his own fragile schemes.

I'm convinced that Sarah got a new husband that day. And Abraham got his family back.

I'm also convinced that this very same event is what changed Sarah. You think about it: With Abraham's track record, would you let him take your boy on a hike with nothing more than a knife and a pile of kindling? No way! That turkey was liable to do just about anything! But when Abraham explained himself, it was like echoes from the past, as she heard him say, *"I don't know where this is leading, Sarah, I don't know where we're supposed to go — but God said to do this, Sarah. And I've messed up for so long, I'm determined this time to do whatever He says."*

And so Sarah, frightened, yet encouraged . . . hopeful, yet still so very afraid . . . allowed that *Failure* the chance to fail one more time. But he didn't. He passed the test. And when Abraham and that boy were seen heading back over the ridge, arm in arm — laughing and crying, joyful and triumphant — there was a change in Sarah's heart. ***AND SHE LEARNED ONCE AGAIN TO RESPOND TO HER HUSBAND WITH A SUBMISSIVE AND SUPPORTIVE SPIRIT.*** And ladies, the Apostle Peter, hundreds of years later, wrote a little footnote intended for you: **"You are her daughters if you do what is right and do not give way to fear"** (1 Pet 3:6).

Then finally, both of them learned that honest communication is the key to marital joy. Affirming words like honesty, sensitivity, and forgiveness returned, while reckless words, destructive words, abusive words — which had so marked their middle years — were stricken from their vocabularies.

No, life did not become for them some stroll through the park. The fact is, Sarah probably always struggled with assertiveness and jealousy. And Abraham was no doubt constantly tempted toward some hair-brained scheme. Both had demonstrated a serious problem with telling the whole truth and nothing but the truth. And yet somehow, in spite of the weaknesses, theirs was a marriage of more than just convenience. It was more than just passing time. In fact, when Sarah died at the age of 127, Abraham could find no consolation. His grief was raw and it was real. He cried for days, we're told. Because the love of his life was gone.

Out of the ashes of failure and desperation, heartache and misery, Abraham and Sarah built a marriage that is held up — all these many years later — as a model for how you and I ought to live. Perfect? No. But a reasonably good marriage that, despite some rough terrain, ended as happily as it had started.

Wounds from Sticks and Stones Heal Better

We began this chapter standing near the base of a large, imposing wall. It's only fitting that we end facing yet another wall. A wall, perhaps, of your own making. A wall, possibly that was built by the sins of your mate — or maybe your own sins. A wall, that, if your marriage is to survive, *must come down.*

Abraham and Sarah found recovery through a crisis. A real life and death situation. The good news is — you don't have to wait for a crisis. You can decide now, in the quiet of your own heart to make a change. To follow God's lead rather than your own plan. Honest communication is the key.

NOTES

[1] Ed Young, *Romancing the Home* (Nashville: Broadman & Holman Publishers, 1993), p. 45.

[2] C.F. Keil and F. Delitzch, *Commentary on the Old Testament*, Volume 1, (Grand Rapids: Eerdmans, n.d.), p. 197.

CHAPTER THREE

Sticking Together When Life Falls Apart
JOB 1–2

Have you ever felt disappointed by God? Perhaps you prayed for something to happen, and, though you fully believed that God was able to do it, that thing never came to be. Maybe you made a major decision, counting on God to come through with the necessary resources, yet those resources never materialized. Philip Yancey tells us that *"disappointment occurs when the actual experience of something falls far short of what we anticipate."*

Have you ever been there? Have you ever been disappointed by God because what you expected Him to do, He did not do?

Maybe you did what you believed was right. You were convinced God wanted you to do it. You didn't want to do it, but believing God was in it, you submitted to His will and did the right thing, anyway, fully expecting that God would then come through with His end of the bargain. But He didn't. You did it God's way, but to no avail. You did right, but it still went wrong. *Have you been there?* Of course you have. And so have I.

I talked with a husband who said, *"Steve, I don't drink, I don't run around, I'm a good provider — yet my wife says she doesn't love me anymore. She wants out. It's been hard, but Steve, I did right by her. Why is this happening?"*

Behind the Tent Flaps

A wife once complained, *"Steve, I loved that man more than life itself. I gave so much to him. Why did he leave?"*

A dear friend lost her husband through cancer. She once told me, *"Our home has always been dedicated to Christ. We had so many plans for investing our lives together in the kingdom. But now I'm alone. I still love the Lord, but I just don't understand."*

A mom said, *"I gave up my career for those kids. I gave them everything I had. But now, they're adults, and neither of them is walking with God. Why? I thought I did it right!"*

I talked with a man who said, *"Steve, I prayed about this business before it even began. At every major point of decision I sought God's counsel. I suppose that's why it's so hard now to let it fail. I followed His leadership, so why didn't this thing succeed?"*

I once talked with two different families, both having moved within several months of each other. One family had a house that hadn't sold. Another family was still emotionally devastated from having been uprooted. Both believed at the time that God was leading them. *"Steve, we prayed about this move! We were convinced that we were doing the right thing! Now look at us!"*

I wonder, do the contents of this letter strike a familiar note in your heart?

> *"Steve, I truly wish I could tell you why I am writing this letter, but I'm not sure myself. Maybe I'm angry and this is a hateful release of some of the feelings I've been harboring. I've gone through cycles . . . almost like a yo-yo of being angry with God, questioning why I am where I am, to beseeching Him to show me some purpose or some good that will come from all of these lives so full of suffering. I have not denied God nor stopped loving Him, but I just can't seem to resolve it all. I do feel that if I died at this moment I would go straight to hell . . . I don't like that feeling, but I have to acknowledge it. I pray, as a very unworthy sinner, that God will direct me in some manner so I can feel there is some purpose to all this suffering. I've prayed for God to numb the pain . . . but so far, He hasn't seen fit to do that. Patience isn't one of my virtues, but 6 years is a long time."*

Sticking Together When Life Falls Apart

The one who penned those lines never signed her name. And, though I wished that I knew who she was, so I could speak to her words of comfort — what do you say when, no matter how hard someone has tried to do it right, it still goes wrong?

A young missionary determined to invest his life in taking the Gospel to the people of Peru. He established a church there, a church that is still thriving today. But sometime after arriving on the field, his six-month old son died from a sudden onset of vomiting and diarrhea. After that, the young missionary's grief seemed beyond recovery. He made a marker by hand from a piece of stone, buried the baby's body, and planted a tree beside the grave. At the hottest part of each day, when everyone else sought shade, the missionary walked to the river and hauled a jug of water and poured it at the base of that tree. Then he stood beside the grave, his shadow falling across it, as if to shield it from the blazing equatorial sun. Sometimes he would weep, sometimes pray, and sometimes just stand there with a vacant gaze. His wife, the Indian church members, and other missionaries all tried to comfort him, but to no avail.

Eventually, the missionary himself got sick. His mind wandered; he had constant diarrhea. He was flown to Lima, where doctors probed him for any sign of amoeba or other tropical organisms — but found nothing. None of the drugs they tried were effective. They diagnosed his problem as *"hysterical diarrhea"* and sent him and his wife back to the States.

When I read that, I wondered what he prayed about as he stood in that blazing heat. No doubt his mind was filled with questions of unfairness. His baby had done nothing wrong. Besides, he brought his family there to serve God — *was this his reward?* He could have stayed back in the States, but he didn't! *Is this the thanks he gets?* His boy is dead! He probably asked God for comfort, but felt none. Until, finally, his body adopted its own coping mechanism — and his entire physical and emotional health vanished.

I suppose this is a problem atheists never have to deal with. An atheist is never disappointed in God. He expects nothing and gets nothing. *But we who commit our lives to Him, who make it our goal to please Him, instinctively expect something in return for that.* Whether we should or not, is another subject. The fact is, we do. And when those expectations don't materialize, WE GET CONFUSED.

And in our confusion, we ask a question. A simple question. A question everyone has asked. *"WHY?" "God, I'm not sure I like the way You're running things right now. Why are you doing this to me?"*

Come with me to the book of Job. Because we're going to pull back the tent flaps once again and peer into the heart of a man who, at first glance it seems, did everything right; and yet the results seemed, at least at first, so very, very wrong. And even though this man was a believer, and his wife also a believer, when they came to the valley of the shadow of death — when the suffering and heartache he faced seemed more than he could possibly bear — it took a toll. Spiritually, emotionally, physically, and even maritally. Job and his wife, in the face of their confusion, in the course of finding no answer to their *'why,'* found what you too have found — that it's really tough to stick together when life seems to be falling apart.

JOB — WHO HE WAS AND WHAT HE FACED

In Job 1, we find yet another honest account of a biblical marriage gone sour. And aren't you glad God is faithful to tell us about these marriages? Don't you find it encouraging that Scripture honestly portrays these spiritual superstars as they really were? Steadfastly refusing to gloss over their obvious and, at times, debilitating frailties? It encourages me. Listen, the losses Job faced were real! And the resultant pain was profound. And, from the human view, there seemed little logic in why it would happen to him. I think that's why Mrs. Job reacted so violently.

But I'm getting ahead of myself. In verses 1-5, we find a brief description of the man Job.

"In the land of Uz there lived a man whose name was Job.

This man was blameless and upright; he feared God and shunned evil" (Job 1:1).

In other words, he was a man who did it right. A man of integrity. A man so genuine in his walk with God that Scripture calls him, **"blameless."**

"He had seven sons and three daughters, and he owned seven thousand sheep, three thousand camels, five hundred yoke of oxen and five hundred donkeys, and had a large number of servants. He was the greatest man among all the people of the East" (Job 1:2-3).

It literally reads, *"he was the heaviest man in the east."* Does that mean he was fat? Not at all. Job was not fat — he was heavy. He was famous. He was rich. He had clout. And yet despite his success in the business world, Job maintained a high priority on family relationships.

"His sons used to take turns holding feasts in their homes, and they would invite their three sisters to eat and drink with them" (Job 1:4).

These ten children are fully grown, yet they still enjoy being together! Evidently, they got together for all the big occasions. Which tells me Mr. and Mrs. Job had done a pretty good job raising those kids. When adult siblings still enjoy getting together, it's a good sign that mom and dad did something right.

"When a period of feasting had run its course, Job would send and have them purified. Early in the morning he would sacrifice a burnt offering for each of them, thinking, 'Perhaps my children have sinned and cursed God in their hearts.' This was Job's regular custom" (Job 1:5).

In other words, long after the kids were grown, Job still practiced a daily intercession on their behalf. He prayed regularly for his kids.

What a guy! Ward Cleaver, if there ever was a Ward Cleaver. A man of no mean reputation, and yet who regarded his family as his first priority. A man who was highly regarded in all the right circles, and yet who had a blameless walk with God. A

Behind the Tent Flaps

dad who never failed to intercede for his adult children.

And yet, suddenly everything changes. According to verse 13, it all happened **"one day."**

But before we read what happened, do you know how you can tell when you're going to have a bad day?

- You can tell it's gonna be a bad day when you see a *60 Minutes* news team waiting in your office.
- You can tell it's gonna be a bad day when you call Suicide Prevention and they put you on hold.
- You can tell it's gonna be a bad day when you turn on the news and they're showing emergency routes out of the city.
- You can tell it's gonna be a bad day when your twin sister forgets your birthday.
- You can tell it's gonna be a bad day when your boss tells you not to bother to take off your coat.
- You can tell it's gonna be a bad day when you call your answering service and they tell you it's none of your business.
- You can tell it's gonna be a bad day when your income tax check bounces.
- You can tell it's gonna be a bad day when you put both contact lenses in the same eye.
- You can tell it's gonna be a bad day when your car horn goes off accidentally and remains stuck as you follow a group of *Hell's Angels* down the expressway.

When that happens, you know — *it's gonna be a bad day!* But Job got no such warning. He awakened that particular morning just as he awakened the day before. There was no angelic messenger who warned him, there was no vision that informed him — nothing! He got up, got dressed, ate breakfast — fully expecting today to be not much different from yesterday.

You see, affliction doesn't make appointments. Remorse refuses to make a reservation. It just happens.

> "One day when Job's sons and daughters were feasting and drinking wine at the oldest brother's house, a messenger came to Job and said, 'The oxen were plowing and the donkeys were grazing nearby, and the Sabeans attacked and carried them off. They put the servants to the sword, and I am the only one who has escaped to tell you!'
> *While he was still speaking,* another messenger came and said, 'The fire of God fell from the sky and burned up the sheep and the servants, and I am the only one who has escaped to tell you!'
> *While he was still speaking,* another messenger came and said, 'The Chaldeans formed three raiding parties and swept down on your camels and carried them off. They put the servants to the sword, and I am the only one who has escaped to tell you!'
> *While he was still speaking,* yet another messenger came and said, 'Your sons and daughters were feasting and drinking wine at the oldest brother's house, when suddenly a mighty wind swept in from the desert and struck the four corners of the house. It collapsed on them and they are dead, and I am the only one who has escaped to tell you!'" (Job 1:13-19, emphasis added).

Not in a matter of months or even weeks, but in a matter of minutes! Job received four back-to-back messages of absolute devastation in rapid-fire succession. He lost his livestock. He lost his servants. He lost a big chunk of his finances. He lost all ten of his children. And it all happened, **"one day."**

It still does. A young husband manages to slip away from the office for a few hours. He races toward home, planning to surprise his wife with an afternoon of romance. Instead, he finds her in bed with another man.

The persistent ringing of the telephone tears through the night, and the voice on the other end says, *"I'm sorry to inform you that Sunset Limited has jumped its tracks, and your daughter and granddaughter have both drowned."*

The physician asks you to come to his office as quickly as possible. You arrive, and he measures his words so very carefully: *"Your biopsy is not good. You have cancer."*

The policeman stands at your door, hat in hand, and finally stammers, *"Your son has been involved in a shooting. He's still alive, but you need to come with me right away."*

Dad and Mom, with grim faces and flat tones, say to you, *"Kids, we've got something we need to tell you. Dad's not going to live here anymore. He's moving out."*

And just like that — in what amounts to hardly a blip on the time line of human history — your whole world comes crashing in.

Mom, I've never been able to tell you, but I'm a homosexual — and I've got AIDS.

Mrs. Smith, your daughter is in a substance abuse center. She's safe, but last night she tried to kill herself.

That's what I call unbearable, unimaginable grief.

JOB — HOW HE RESPONDED AND WHAT CAME NEXT

For the life of me, I cannot enter into Job's pain. Here's a man, who, in addition to his cattle and his servants and his livelihood, lost all ten of his children. *HOW DID JOB RESPOND?* Satan maintained that he would curse God. That's why this whole scene happened. Satan was trying to prove his point. He maintained that the only reason Job was good is because life was good. *Make his life bad, and Job will curse you!*

Did Job curse God?

"At this, Job got up and tore his robe and shaved his head" (Job 1:20a).

In other words, he grieved. He tore his robe as a sign of the tearing of his heart. He shaved his head as if to say, *"I have lost everything of value to me."*

"Then he fell to the ground . . ." (Job 1:20b).

I picture him just slumping to his knees. So stricken with heartache that he didn't even have enough strength to support his own weight. He just fell to the ground . . .

"**. . . in worship**" (Job 1:20c).

He worshiped? Yes, he worshiped. He expresses no cynicism, he refuses to succumb to cursing, he raises no fist toward the heavens — this is a picture of abject humility.

One commentator writes, *"Behold the wise man Job! Not wise because he comprehended the mystery of his suffering — but because while not comprehending it, he worshipped God anyway."* In other words, even though Job couldn't make sense of all this — even though he knew he had done right, yet life had gone so wrong, even though the 'whys' were swimming about his entire conscious mind — he still had the presence of mind to say . . .

"'Naked I came from my mother's womb, and naked I will depart. The LORD** gave and the L**ORD** has taken away; may the name of the L**ORD** be praised'"** (Job 1:21).

Several years ago, my phone rang at about 3 o'clock in the morning. I reached for the receiver and heard Bill's voice at the other end. He said, *"Steve, the babies were just delivered. Carol's doing fine, but the girls are being rushed to Children's Hospital. It doesn't look like the little one's going to make it."*

I arrived just moments after she was pronounced dead. Bill took me by the arm and led me to a shadowy, empty waiting room, and said, *"Steve, we need to pray."* Twelve days later, the other baby also died. I wondered what I would say. I prayed for wisdom. I sought direction for what I could possibly say to these two dear people. When the elevator door opened, there they stood. I looked into their tear-stained eyes and opened my mouth — but nothing came. Bill put his hand on my shoulder, and he said, *"Steve, the Lord is the strength of my life."* And I knew in that moment that I was in the presence of greatness. Here was a man, like Job, who knew the score.

Did Job grieve? You bet he did. *Was he dealing with reality?* Yeah. *Was he put together different than me?* No. He was a man just like us. It's just that his eyes were so unswervingly on the

Lord, that not even this tragedy could draw him aside.

"In all this, Job did not sin by charging God with wrongdoing" (Job 1:22).

Now you'd think that after such a wonderful response as that, things would start to go better for Job. I mean, hasn't he had enough? I talked with a woman once who said, *"Steve, it's just one thing right after another! I handle this crisis, and just about the time I think I've got it together — here comes another crisis!"* That's probably how Job felt, too.

"So Satan went out from the presence of the LORD **and afflicted Job with painful sores from the soles of his feet to the top of his head"** (Job 2:7).

The word literally refers to skin ulcers. Boils. You don't hear so much about boils these days, but when I was a kid, I remember my dad, a minister, had a boil on the back of his neck. And it was so painful; it caused such agony that he had to do one Sunday's service in a T-shirt. But Job had those "little nasties" *all over his body!* From the top of his head, to the soles of his feet. And the only relief he could find was when he . . .

". . . took a piece of broken pottery and scraped himself with it as he sat among the ashes" (Job 2:8).

Chapter 7 tells us that they robbed him of his sleep. And then, when he did sleep, he had nightmares! *Can you imagine?*

JOB'S WIFE — HOW SHE REACTED AND WHAT SHE SAID

And it was at that point that MRS. JOB had had it. She helplessly watched as her suffering spouse scraped his skin in search of solace. She, too, was grappling with the grief which gripped her heart. And in her mind, enough was enough. She said to him:

"Are you still holding on to your integrity? Curse God and die!" (Job 2:9).

One commentator writes:

It is doubtful whether anyone was ever placed before a severer trial than was Job. God allowed Satan to take everything away from him that could possibly have been a source of encouragement to him. And when Satan had robbed him of all these things, he permitted him to keep what most grieved him. Satan permitted Job's wife to live. *If the Devil had supposed that the slightest semblance of comfort might have been given Job by his wife, he would certainly have robbed him of her.* But Satan knew he could use her as an instrument with which to grieve and torture his victim, and for that reason he permitted her to live.

The best commentators have always interpreted Satan's actions and the character of Job's wife in this way. Long ago, Augustine spoke of her as the *"Devil's accomplice,"* and Calvin did not hesitate to call her *"an instrument of Satan"* and a *"diabolical fury."* Pseudo-gallantry and sentimentality have attempted to furbish her dull finish, but the attempts have failed. The words she spoke to Job can not be erased, and the poignant significance of these cannot be distorted.

Faith's bow had been drawn to the breaking point in Job's heart. A hairs-breadth of added exertion, it seemed, would cause it to snap. Job was at the point of surrendering to Satan. He was tortured by physical pains and tantalized by spiritual griefs. At this moment his wife visited him as he sat upon the heap of ashes. She refused to give him the slightest hint of encouragement. She did not even reveal a token of ordinary human sympathy. Instead, she diabolically urged him to relinquish his faith in God and to end his suffering by suicide.[1]

Now I'm not thrilled with what Mrs. Job had to say. It's obvious that what Job needed most from his wife was sensitive support. What he got instead was critical counsel. She's the only one in the entire book who brings up the subject of suicide. But the fact is, she just lost ten children, too. And when you go through that kind of grief, you tend to say things that are wrong. And if you deny that, you have never grieved.

This woman is in misery. And in her misery, she offers to her husband bad counsel. It was the wrong thing to say. But remember the words of George Washington Carver? He said that we need to be *"sympathetic with the striving."* And if anyone was striving, it was Mrs. Job. Ten fresh graves stared at her from a nearby field. Her husband is a fiery mass of oozing, itching boils. No wonder she told him to just end it all!

Job replied:

> **"You are talking like a foolish woman. Shall we accept good from God, and not trouble?"** (Job 2:10).

There you have it. There's the explanation you've been looking for. *How is it that Job could handle this affliction? How is it that he could actually worship on this, the most horrific day of his life?* It's because Job's God is not just a kind-hearted Santa Claus Who only gives good things. He is a God Who gives to His children those gifts which will bring ultimate glory to Himself. And that includes blessing, but it also includes adversity. Job understood that. And so he accepted, with humility and grace, whatever God chose to bring his way.

I have a question for those who are wives: *Ladies, do you realize how important your counsel is to your husband?* If you've married a strong, silent type — you may not have a clue. But my guess is, your counsel is more significant than you may realize.

In 1849 when Nathaniel Hawthorne was dismissed from his government job in the customshouse, he went home in despair. His wife listened to his tale of woe, sat pen and ink on the table before him, lit the fire, put her arms around his shoulders, and said, *"Now you will be able to write your novel."* He did, and the result was that great American classic, *The Scarlet Letter.*

There was a time in Martin Luther's life when he was desperately depressed. He refused to eat, he refused to drink, he refused to speak to his wife, his children or even his dearest friend. It was at that point that Catherine, his wife, put on her widow's garments and assumed the position of a person in deepest mourning. Surprised, Luther asked, *"Why are you sorrowing?"* To which she replied, *"Dear Doctor, I have cause for the saddest of weeping, for God in his heaven has died."* That tender, very gentle rebuke hit its mark. With a laugh, Luther kissed her, took courage, and joy returned to that house.

Sticking Together When Life Falls Apart

Joni Eareckson Tada tells us that approximately 75 percent of all marriages break up when the home is invaded with the pressures brought on by some form of lingering suffering — be it a physical handicap, a mental deficiency, some type of developmental disability, or even the loss of a child through death. Marital conflict is common in homes which have experienced some form of tragedy.

One reason, in my view, is that the pain is so great — that both mates are so busy salving their own wounds — they lose all sense of compassion for their mate's wounds. I sense that was the case with Mrs. Job. She's hurting so badly, without any thought for her husband — she just blurts it out! She wasn't trying to be cruel, but because her words were so sharp, it *was* cruel.

What her husband needed was encouragement, not desperation. He needed a cheerleader, not a critic. And yet, the only other counsel she gave her man was in Job 19:17, when Job admits, **"My breath is offensive to my wife."** Isn't that something? He's sitting there in absolute agony, reeking with the stench of death, his body wracked with unbelievable pain — and she has the audacity to complain about his breath? *Give me a break!*

Which reminds me of the time a woman in our church told her husband that she was pregnant again, and within days he was gone. Or the time in another ministry, when the wife contracted cancer, and her husband, claiming that he could not bear to see her suffer, raced into the arms of another woman.

Hey, everybody needs a cheerleader. Especially when things are going bad. Sometimes it's just the roar of the crowd that propels the home team to victory. Sometimes it's the affirming nod from your dear companion that gives you the courage to stay the course. Job got neither.

Marabel Morgan tells of the time Bob Griese threw a pass to Paul Warfield, who ran more than forty yards to score the game-winning touchdown just as time expired. After he spiked the ball, he ran along the sidelines, as 60,000 fans leaped to their feet cheering and screaming and singing and hugging!

But Warfield's eyes were still searching the stands for his wife. When their eyes met, he waved, and she smiled, and gave him a thumbs up! And that's all he needed. Forget the 60,000 fans. Only one person's approval really mattered.

I understand that. When I'm preaching, I am more on my toes, I feel most strongly energized when my wife, Vanessa, is in the audience. Now understand, I give it everything I've got every time I preach. But, quite honestly, I think I do better when she's around. And even if everyone else says something nice about my sermon — until she says something, it's not enough. I long for her praise and recognition. And she longs for that from me, too.

JOB'S FRIENDS — WHY THEY VISITED AND WHAT THEY ASSUMED

Mrs. Job blew it. I understand why — but she still blew it.

So did Job's friends. True, things went well at first.

> "When Job's three friends, Eliphaz the Temanite, Bildad the Shuhite, and Zophar the Naamathite, heard about all the troubles that had come upon him, they set out from their homes and met together by agreement to go and sympathize with him and comfort him. When they saw him from a distance, they could hardly recognize him; they began to weep aloud, and they tore their robes and sprinkled dust on their heads. Then they sat on the ground with him for seven days and seven nights. No one said a word to him, because they saw how great his suffering was" (Job 2:11-13).

And if only they had left after verse 13, their ministry would have been a great encouragement. But they didn't. For whatever reason, they thought they had to say something wise.

Do you have a friend right now who's going through a really bad time? Don't feel like you have to be insightful. Don't go to him armed with three cliches, four pieces of advice and seven Scripture verses — just go to him, and, in silence, share in his sorrow. Just being there is what matters. The best grief ministry

I know is a soft hug, a kind look and a gentle touch. And that's what these gave Job for seven wonderfully encouraging days.

HOWEVER! Once they started talking? Once they started searching for answers as to why this was happening? It was awful! They erroneously concluded that Job was suffering because Job was bad. Now, Job wasn't *perfect*, but Job also knew — Job wasn't bad. He was a good man. He had done a lot of things right — yet life still went very, very wrong. *Listen, you don't have any idea why it is that someone else is suffering. So keep it to yourself.*

THE FINALE — WHAT JOB LEARNED AND WHAT THE LORD DID

Because these "counselors" obviously had nothing of value to share, let's just skip all of that nonsense — and instead, let's take a look at a couple of lessons that Job learned from all of this.

First, Job learned that suffering is an essential part of God's plan. He learned that there is a positive benefit to heartache. Over in Job 5, he writes:

> "Blessed is the man whom God corrects; so do not despise the discipline of the Almighty. For he wounds, but he also binds up; he injures, but his hands also heal. From six calamities he will rescue you; in seven no harm will befall you. In famine he will ransom you from death, and in battle from the stroke of the sword. You will be protected from the lash of the tongue, and need not fear when destruction comes. You will laugh at destruction and famine, and need not fear the beasts of the earth" (Job 5:17-22).

And he goes on, describing in detail the strength that comes from suffering. In much the same spirit that James employs when he writes, **"Consider it pure joy, my brothers, whenever you face trials of many kinds"** (James 1:2). Joy? Yes, joy. **"Because you know that the testing of your faith develops perseverance"** (James 1:3).

And throughout Scripture, the testimony is always the same. *Suffering develops faith.* I'm generally a much stronger person when I have endured a tragedy. *Suffering enhances my character.* It helps me in my personal development. *Suffering prepares me to minister to others.* Haven't you found that to be true? Those who *have* suffered minister best to those who *are* suffering. *Suffering exposes sin and personal weakness,* as in the case of Mrs. Job. *Suffering helps bring me to maturity.*

It's essential, friend, that you and I suffer. You may not like that, you may try to resist its reality — but it is hurt that opens the heart. It's the strong winds which cause my roots to grow deep.

Bob Benson had a friend who had a very serious heart attack. For a while it didn't look like he would live. But he improved enough to undergo the surgery that, in time, gave him a new lease on life. Months later, Benson asked him,

"W.T., how did you like your heart attack?"
"It scared me to death — almost."
"Would you like to do it again?"
"NO!"
"Would you recommend it?"
"Definitely not!"
"Wait a minute, does your life mean more to you now than it did before?"
"Well, yes."
"You and Nell have always had a good marriage, but you're closer than ever now, aren't you?"
"Yes."
"How about your new granddaughter?"
"Did I show you her picture?"
"Yes. W.T., You seem to have a new compassion for people . . . a deeper understanding and sympathy . . ."
"Yes."
"And you've said that you know the Lord in a richer, deeper fellowship than you had ever thought possible?"
"Yes."
"So, how did you like your heart attack?"[2]

Silence was his answer. It's true: suffering is an essential part of God's plan.

Job also learned that *sovereign is who God is*. Job, in the midst of his confusion, his anxiety, and his heartache, experiences a powerful moment of inspiration.

> "But if I go to the east, he is not there; if I go to the west, I do not find him. When he is at work in the north, I do not see him; when he turns to the south, I catch no glimpse of him" (Job 23:8-9).

If you've ever really suffered, you know Job's plight. *God, where are you?*

> "But he knows the way that I take; when he has tested me, I will come forth as gold. My feet have closely followed his steps; I have kept to his way without turning aside. I have not departed from the commands of his lips; I have treasured the words of his mouth more than my daily bread. But he stands alone, and who can oppose him? He does whatever he pleases. He carries out his decree against me, and many such plans he still has in store" (Job 23:10-14).

My friend, when you come to the end, this is the passage that you ought to read. *God will do as He pleases! He will not be opposed. What He has decreed will happen*. But there's an end to it. And when I have completed the test, **"I will come forth as gold."** But remember it well — God will have His way.

In Isaiah 45 the prophet writes:

> "I am the LORD, and there is no other; apart from me there is no God. I will strengthen you, though you have not acknowledged me, so that from the rising of the sun to the place of its setting men may know there is none besides me. I am the LORD, and there is no other. I form the light and create darkness, I bring prosperity and create disaster; I, the LORD, do all these things" (Isa 45:5-7).

There's no hedging here. God isn't hiding under a rock hoping that you won't blame Him for your pain. He says, *"It's My responsibility! I do that! And I do it for your good and and for My glory! I know what you can handle, and so I send it your way. Not to crush you, but to empower you. I know the strength that you possess, and so I increase your burden, taking joy in your willingness to carry it. I am God, Isaiah, and there is no explaining Me. Sometimes there is no answer to the WHY. Except that if you receive from me the good things — why don't you also receive from me what you perceive as bad? I love you, and this thing in your life is designed to do a work in you that could be done in no other way. So just trust Me to do what is best."*

Job 42. The end has come. And the first thing God does is discipline Job's counselors. Take a look:

> "After the LORD had said these things to Job, he said to Eliphaz the Temanite, 'I am angry with you and your two friends, because you have not spoken of me what is right, as my servant Job has'" (Job 42:7).

Wow! That ought to strike fear in the heart of every would-be counselor! Christian, before you quickly give advice to your hurting friend, before you say, *"Well, here's what I would do . . ."* make sure that what you are about to speak is **"right."** Say, *"God, guide my lips! Don't let me say something stupid!"*

It was then that the Lord turned his attention to Job.

> "After Job had prayed for his friends, the LORD made him prosperous again and gave him twice as much as he had before. All his brothers and sisters and everyone who had known him before came and ate with him in his house. They comforted and consoled him over all the trouble the LORD had brought upon him, and each one gave him a piece of silver and a gold ring. The LORD blessed the latter part of Job's life more than the first. He had fourteen thousand sheep, six thousand camels, a thousand yoke of oxen and a thousand donkeys. And he also had seven sons and three daughters" (Job 42:10-13).

Someone has said that the reason he didn't double his children is — well, that would be a curse, not a blessing.

> "After this, Job lived a hundred and forty years; he saw his children and their children to the fourth generation. And so he died, old and full of years." (Job 42:16-17).

Sticking Together When Life Falls Apart

So how do you stick together when life is falling apart?

I love the story of the two "good ol' boys" who went deer hunting. They dropped an eleven-point buck and were proudly dragging it through the underbrush toward their truck. They encountered another hunter who said, *"Fellas, it's none of my business, but if you'll pull that deer by the horns instead of the legs, his horns won't get caught in the underbrush. Beside, he'll be lots easier to pull!"* Recognizing the man's wisdom, they dropped the deer's legs, grabbed him by the horns, and started pulling. After a couple of minutes, the first guy said, "That stranger sure was smart. This deer's a whole lot easier to pull." The other "good ol' boy" said, *"Yeah, but we're getting farther from the truck all the time!"*

I know, it's a stupid joke. But it's not a joke how many husbands and wives draw further and further apart because they lose sight of their goal. They forget that they exist to glorify God, and, as Job put it in chapter 2, that they ought to willingly receive whatever He chooses to give, whether good or bad. In forgetting, they get further and further away from where they'd really like to be. They drift away from each other and from God.

The key to sticking together when life falls apart is to say, *"God, whatever you choose to bring my way, I will accept it. And help me remember, Lord, that nothing will happen to me that You and I together cannot handle."*

The world renowned theologian, Dolly Parton, once said that if you want the rainbow, you have to put up with the rain. She's right. It takes rain to make a rainbow. And in life, it takes dark times to enhance the good times; it takes sorrow to bring meaning to our joy. And in those rare lives where adversity is missing — joy is not nearly as deep, laughter does not ring nearly as true, faith does not run nearly so deep.

Now it's true: Suffering can make you better or it can make you bitter. It can drive you and your mate apart or it can drive you even closer together. It can fill your heart with anger and resentment and hostility, or — as Isaiah tells us — it can fill your heart with peace. He said to the Lord, **"God, You will keep in perfect peace him whose mind is steadfast, because he trusts in you"** (Isa 26:3).

I know that there are many who read this book who are suffering. And if it were up to me, I would wave a magical wand and all of your pain would vanish. But then again, that wouldn't necessarily be the best thing, would it? I mean, not if I really believe what I've just written. No, if I really believe even in pain there is profit . . . that even in grief there is gain — that our God works all things, even hurtful things, to accomplish ultimate and eternal good — if we believe that, then we must humbly accept whatever His hand provides.

Laura Barker struck a chord in my heart when she wrote:

"My child, I have a message for you today. Let Me tell you that it may gild with glory any storm clouds that may arise and smooth the rough places upon which you may have to tread. It's short, only five words, but let them sink into your inmost souls. Use them as a pillow upon which to rest your weary head. THIS THING IS FROM ME.

Have you ever thought of it, that all that concerns you, concerns Me, too? Therefore, it is My special delight to educate you. I would have you learn when temptations assail you and the enemy comes in like a flood, that THIS THING IS FROM ME.

That your weakness needs My might and your safety lies in letting Me fight for you. Are you in difficult circumstances surrounded by people who don't understand you, who never consult your taste, who put you on the back burner? THIS THING IS FROM ME.

I'm the God of all circumstances. Thou camest not to this place by accident. It is the very place I meant you to be. Have you asked to be made humble? THIS THING IS FROM ME.

Are you in money difficulties? THIS THING IS FROM ME.

Are you passing through the night of sorrow? THIS THING IS FROM ME.

This day I place in your hand — this pot of holy oil — make use of it freely, my child. Let every circumstance that arises, every word that pains you, every interruption that would make you impatient, every revelation of your witness

— every groaning of your soul, be anointed with this oil. The sting will go as you learn, THIS THING IS FROM ME."

NOTES

[1]Abraham Kuyper, *Women of the Old Testament* (Grand Rapids: Zondervan, 1993), pp. 133-134.

[2]Bob Benson, *See You at the House* (Nashville: Generoux Nelson, 1989), pp. 241-242.

CHAPTER FOUR

One Night of Ecstasy, A Whole Lifetime of Agony
2 SAMUEL 11–18

Erma Bombeck writes:

Just when you think you've heard every far-out story ever pitched in Hollywood, along comes *"Indecent Proposal,"* the story of a billionaire who offers $1 million to sleep with a man's wife.

I didn't have enough on my mind worrying about Bosnia, Mia and Woody, and crime in Miami. Now I have to think about what to do if faced with an infidelity lottery.

Frankly, the concept has shaken up the entire married community. It's what all couples are talking about. Not since Michael Douglas and Glenn Close in *"Fatal Attraction"* forced us to consider the pitfalls of adultery have we dissected our relationships so intensely.

There isn't a woman alive who doesn't secretly wonder how her spouse would react to the proposal. As my husband dozed in his chair, I kicked his foot and asked, *"Would you consider sharing me for a million bucks?"*

He was silent for a moment. *"Are we talking about cash or check?"*

"What difference does it make?" I shouted. *"You've missed the point. This isn't Ed McMahon with a Publishers' Clearinghouse winner. This is a man buying your wife!"*

He said, *"Would we be having this conversation if the billionaire looked like Ernest Borgnine?"*

"Redford isn't the issue here," I lied. *"The money is."*

"How did he find out about you in the first place? Is this a random sleepover?"

"I don't know! It's all just hypothetical."

"Then why is it important to know? Tell me when the offer is firm."

I stared at Redford's picture that topped the story I was reading. *"Everyone could use a million dollars,"* I said wistfully. *"Of course, I'd give the money to the President to apply to the national debt."*

"How about the orphanage?" smiled my husband.

"The orphanage is good."

"Now I know what this is all about," he said. *"It's a reprise on the old theme, 'Do you still love me?'"*

"If men would say it more often, we wouldn't have to set you up," I snapped.

"We had this same conversation when Bette Midler was kidnapped in a film and ransomed, and they marked her down."

"You're just teasing," I said. *"You wouldn't share me for a million dollars . . . or 2 million or 3 million. Would you?"*

I should have known better than to throw that many zeroes at a man who needs a new transmission.

So how about it? *Would you do it?* I mean, really. Transmission or not — *would you take the bait and make the deal?* Man! What a loaded question. **What price fidelity?**

Now before you answer, I want to introduce you to a man who not only would — he did. Except that he didn't do it for money — he did it for pure, unabashed pleasure. And what did he get for his trouble? HE GOT ONE NIGHT OF ECSTASY, BUT A WHOLE LIFETIME OF AGONY.

I'm speaking, of course, of **David**, the humble shepherd boy who became a king. The noted singer and songwriter who was equally famous for his conquests on the field of battle. **David**, the righteous king of Israel — the only man of whom it was said that he was a man after God's **"own heart."** (See 1 Sam 13:14; Acts 13:22.) And yet — David blew it. Royally. This otherwise godly king had a moral lapse one night — and in those few hours of compromise, he committed what has become the most notorious sin since Eve bit the apple.

One Night of Ecstasy, A Whole Lifetime of Agony

THE NIGHT OF ECSTASY

By the time we come to 2 Samuel 11, David is about 50 years old. He has sat on Israel's throne for some two decades now and has distinguished himself throughout the known world as a valiant warrior and a visionary leader. He has led his people in righteousness — and has modeled before them a wonderful spirit of praise and worship. In all the world, there was not another king like Israel's king.

I mention that for a reason. I take the time to rehearse David's impeccable record because I'm building a case. Because it would be very easy to focus on 2 Samuel 11, review David's infamous exploit with Bathsheba, and, when we're through, mistakenly assume that Israel's king was a pervert. Some morally depraved reprobate. An evil, despicable, subhuman cad. When the truth is, he was none of the above.

Now David was no angel either. He was a great man, but a man nonetheless. He was a man of no small strength — but make no mistake: *He had chinks in his armor just as you and I have chinks in our armor.* Chinks that unavoidably led to that ill-fated night of ecstasy. *What were these chinks?*

Well, Scripture doesn't give them a lot of air time, but looking through the lens of the past, we find, for one, that *DAVID HAD DEMONSTRATED AN INSATIABLE APPETITE FOR LUST.* According to Deuteronomy 17, there were three things which were to mark the life of Israel's king.

> "When you enter the land the LORD your God is giving you and have taken possession of it and settled in it, and you say, 'Let us set a king over us like all the nations around us, be sure to appoint over you the king the LORD your God chooses" (Deut 17:14-15a).

With that as the base, here are the three things Israel's king must never do (Deut 17:16-17).

> *#1: "The king, moreover, must not acquire great numbers of horses for himself or make the people return to Egypt to get more of them, for the LORD has told you, 'You are not to go back that way again.'"*

Behind the Tent Flaps

#2: *"He must not take many wives, or his heart will be led astray."*

#3: *"He must not accumulate large amounts of silver and gold."*

Of interest to us is requirement #2. It seems that David fulfilled #1 and #3, but in regard to having many wives? David had been an obvious failure. I say that because 2 Samuel 5:12-13 said it first:

> "And David knew that the LORD had established him as king over Israel and had exalted his kingdom for the sake of his people Israel. After he left Hebron, David took more concubines and wives in Jerusalem, and more sons and daughters were born to him" (2 Sam 5:12-13).

In other words, he increased the size of his harem. He added a few more wives, then complemented the wives with some more concubines. We don't know how many — but any was too many! For "any" was a direct disobedience to God's command!

David had an extremely active (can there be any doubt?) libido. One woman was just not enough for him. Nor two. Not even three. Nor 23! So in some vain attempt to satisfy his craving, David had created a monster. And that's the way it always is. If you feed your lust — if you pander to your sexual appetite — what you will get for your trouble is an even more demanding passion. Lust, by its very nature, refuses to be satisfied.

Now you can bet that not just a few folks in Israel noticed this not so subtle compromise. They saw the crack in his character, *but how do you confront a king*? Especially a king with a resumé like David's! And so, for nearly twenty years, David nursed what seemed to be a harmless little quirk — a quirk that in time would clean his clock!

Chapter 11 gives us insight into a second chink. Up until this time in David's life, he had been actively involved in the conquests of Israel. He loved the thrill of military engagement. Remember that scene in the movie *Patton?* General George S. Patton stands on a knoll overlooking a field strewn with smok-

One Night of Ecstasy, A Whole Lifetime of Agony

ing vehicles, wrecked equipment, staggering soldiers, and, as he surveyed the scene, said to himself, *". . . how I love it!"* That's David. And yet . . .

> **"In the spring, at the time when kings go off to war, David sent Joab out with the king's men and the whole Israelite army"** (2 Sam 11:1a).

The army dutifully fulfilled its objectives — pillaging and plundering . . .

> **"They destroyed the Ammonites and besieged Rabbah.** [However . . .] **But David remained in Jerusalem"** (2 Sam 11:1b).

Prior to this moment, David's bio sketch revealed the ultimate success story. With the touch of Midas, it seemed that whatever David handled turned to gold. He was rich beyond measure, he possessed power without peer, he was known throughout the world as *the most enviable man on the planet!*

I suppose you can't blame him for backing away. If anyone deserved some time off — it was David. Maybe it *was* time for the young whippersnappers to assume the sword.

The trouble is, David was still a mover and shaker at heart. So he busied himself doing nothing — he gave himself just as emphatically to the pursuit of personal pleasure and happiness as he had before given himself to his accumulation of power and prestige — and Satan found in David's heart fertile soil for the seed of compromise.

Let that be fair warning to you who are successful. To you who have enjoyed a life of accomplishment and effectiveness. To you who are beginning to think, *"I've put in my time. Now it's time to think about me."* **Beware!** For in the backwash of such thinking resides a vulnerable heart. Mark it well: Life's greatest battles do not generally attack when your nose is to the grindstone. It's when you've got time on your hands and you're bored — that's when the battle strikes.

If you don't believe me, ask David. Here was a successful, extremely powerful man who had an obvious problem with lust. And it's springtime — the time of romance and love — so

Behind the Tent Flaps

David decides that it's also time to indulge himself a bit. So he opts for the bedroom instead of the battlefield.

I take it from verse 2 that he was having some trouble falling asleep one night, so he kicked back the covers and decided to take a stroll on the roof. The palace was an elegant, out-of-the-way patio of sorts where kings would enjoy private leisure with the family. It was ancient Israel's Camp David.

"One evening David got up from his bed and walked around on the roof of the palace" (2 Sam 11:2a).

I picture him leaning on the rail and gazing out across the lights of the city when all of a sudden — he heard the sound of splashing water. He turned, and . . .

"From the roof he saw a woman bathing. The woman was very beautiful . . ." (2 Sam 11:2b).

I love the honesty of Scripture, don't you? Bathsheba was a babe! Drop-dead gorgeous was what she was!

Some questions inevitably arise. *How come David chose **this** time not to go to battle? Was it because all of a sudden he was too old? Too important? Too lazy?* Or could it be that David stayed home because he had already laid out a carefully devised provision for satisfying his flesh? Honestly, I find it hard to believe that he just took a walk, saw a woman and blew it. I think he'd been staking her out for some time. He knew her bathing routine. So he waited until her warrior husband left town with the troops, and then he decided to just sit this battle out and stay home! He had planned, all along, to take a walk on the roof. And, lo and behold, there she was!

And what about Bathsheba? What's she doing taking a bath on her roof? Pardon my suspicious mind, but, living as close to the palace as Bathsheba obviously lived, don't you think she had noticed the king taking these evening walks? Really! If you lived by the most famous man in the world, wouldn't you buy a set of binoculars? I would! And if that's the case — if she knew that David could possibly see her, too — why didn't Bathsheba draw the shades? I personally believe that she actually positioned the tub in the precise location where David couldn't *possibly* miss her.

Now understand, I'm not trying to let David off the hook. He's the one who sinned and, as we will see, he paid an awful price for what he did. All I'm trying to say is that Bathsheba was culpable, too. Why, she played to his weakness! Any woman worth her salt knows full well that a man is stimulated by what he sees. A guy can see a woman in the mall and, without knowing anything about her, he's aroused. He can drive by a billboard going 73 miles per hour and get turned on by the Coppertone model sprawled on her blanket! That doesn't mean men are animals, mind you — it's just the way we were made! *Knowing that, as I'm convinced that she did, why was Bathsheba so careless?*

If only David had gone to war, he would not have seen her. If only she had carefully considered her actions, the temptation would never have happened. Instead, David is now leaning even further over the railing, and his motor starts racing. His heart starts pounding. His palms start sweating, and — in that moment of smoldering desire and fever-pitched passion — he falls.

By the way, Scripture is quite clear in its counsel to those who are so tempted. It can be summed up in one word: *FLEE!* When you stare lust right in the eyes, the Bible says — *GET OUT!* 1 Corinthians 6:18 says: **"Flee from sexual immorality."** 1 Corinthians 10:14 says: **"Flee from idolatry."** 2 Timothy 2:22 says: **"Flee the evil desires of youth."** 2 Peter 1:4 says: **"Escape [flee] the corruption in the world."** It is not a sign of courage that you're willing to stand in there and take the heat. When you are under the gun of a temptation toward lust — the true sign of courage is to run.

But David didn't run, he looked.

He did more than look, he stared.

He did more than stare, he gawked.

And he became so enraptured by Bathsheba's beauty that he . . .

Behind the Tent Flaps

". . . sent someone to find out about her. The man said, 'Isn't this Bathsheba, the daughter of Eliam and the wife of Uriah the Hittite?'" (2 Sam 11:3).

Time out! That's anything but a typical Jewish genealogy. Ordinarily, such a report included a person's parents and grandparents. But this servant adds, *"She's married, David. She's got a husband. He's one of your soldiers. Back off!"* I really think he knew what the king had in mind. He'd seen David's flirtatious ways. He'd been with David on royal jaunts before. He'd seen David look at a woman and decide that he just had to have her! He knew the signs. And so, like a good friend, he gently warned him.

And, thank the Lord, sometimes when we're tempted? God will graciously send a reminder to try to turn us aside, too. Maybe it's the counsel of a friend. Maybe it's the interruption of your plans. Maybe it's a sermon or a song. Some last-minute alarm goes off, urging you to give it up.

The problem is, David had been toying with this for too long. Lust was ruling his heart, and no matter what the price — nothing else mattered but being with her.

"Then David sent messengers to get her. She came to him, and he slept with her" (2 Sam 11:4a).

That's why I say Bathsheba was guilty. There's no sign of a struggle. No hint that she feigned some kind of false modesty.

He sent for her . . .

She came . . .

They slept together.

You may disagree, but I rather think they were pretty cavalier about the whole deal!

"Then she went back home" (2 Sam 11:4b).

No doubt they rationalized their actions. Bathsheba probably complained that her husband didn't love her like she needed to be loved. And David probably said something like, *"My 57 wives don't understand me."*

One Night of Ecstasy, A Whole Lifetime of Agony

And if you don't think David enjoyed this forbidden encounter, you're kidding yourself. The Bible freely admits that sin brings pleasure, **"for a short time"** (Heb 11:25).

However, long after the pleasure was gone — Bathsheba picked up the phone, and spoke those three words every promiscuous fornicator dreads to hear: **"I am pregnant."**

You know what I think when I read that? *Satan doesn't play fair.* He shows you the beautiful body, he describes to you the astounding pleasure, he paints visual fantasies that lure you right into his trap. But he *doesn't* tell you that if you drink and drive — you could kill your own son. That if you become a compulsive gambler — you could lose your home. That if you play around sexually — you could get AIDS . . . and you could die. It's only after you take the bait that the bills come due!

And just like that — *The Ecstasy Is Over And The Agony Begins.*

THE LIFETIME OF AGONY

Now understand, David still could've recovered from this. Adultery is *not* the unpardonable sin. I fully believe that if he had called his cabinet together and told them of his sin, and if he had openly admitted his guilt before the people — that a whole lifetime of agony could have been avoided. God would have still dealt with him, but the consequences would certainly have been far less than what he endured.

However, instead of coming clean and taking his licks like a man — David tried to cover his tracks.

"David sent this word to Joab: 'Send me Uriah the Hittite.' And Joab sent him to David. When Uriah came to him, David asked him how Joab was, how the soldiers were and how the war was going" (2 Sam 11:6-7).

I'm convinced that this was the first time Uriah had even met the King. Yet David is so concerned about his deeds, that he's actually trying to make small-talk with an underling? No doubt Uriah was wondering, *Why did he send for me? What have I done wrong?* Not you, Uriah. You didn't do anything wrong.

Behind the Tent Flaps

How does David explain this strange chain of events? Uriah had dirty feet! That's why he needed to come home and have a personal audience with the king!

> **"Then David said to Uriah, 'Go down to your house and wash your feet'"** (2 Sam 11:8a).

Now you know the score. David didn't care about Uriah's feet. He wanted Uriah to lay with his wife! But things didn't go quite as David had planned.

> **"Uriah left the palace, and a gift from the king was sent after him. But Uriah slept at the entrance to the palace with all his master's servants and did not go down to his house. When David was told, 'Uriah did not go home,' he asked him, 'Haven't you just come from a distance? Why didn't you go home?'"** (2 Sam 11:8b-10).

I wanted you to go home! Now get this:

> **"Uriah said to David, 'The ark and Israel and Judah are staying in tents, and my master Joab and my lord's men are camped in the open fields. How could I go to my house to eat and drink and lie with my wife? As surely as you live, I will not do such a thing!'"** (2 Sam 11:11).

How could I even think about giving myself such pleasure when my buddies are still in the trenches? King, that would be wrong! That would be selfish! I couldn't put my pleasure above the needs of my troops! Thwapp! Right in David's heart! And even though David threw a party and got the man stone-drunk — not even then did he go home to be with his wife! He slept on those steps a second time, to the absolute bewilderment of his King. Isn't that hilarious? David had quite a way with the women — but he couldn't do a thing with this man!

Now understand, abortion was not an option. Had this thing happened in our day, David would have shoved a few shekels in Bathsheba's hands and hustled her over to some clinic in Nineveh. But because abortion lacked its present "acceptability" and ease of access, David decided to murder the husband instead of the baby.

He tried to make it appear legitimate. He even wrote a letter to his trusted crony, Joab, ordering him to . . .

One Night of Ecstasy, A Whole Lifetime of Agony

"'Put Uriah in the front line where the fighting is fiercest. Then withdraw from him so he will be struck down and die'" (2 Sam 11:15).

And that's exactly what happened. And the anxiously anticipated word was quickly received: **". . . your servant Uriah the Hittite is dead"** (2 Sam 11:24).

"When Uriah's wife heard that her husband was dead, she mourned for him. After the time of mourning was over, David had her brought to his house . . ." (2 Sam 11:26-27a).

Look at that! The corpse is barely cold, and David had Bathsheba move in with him! And that's not all!

". . . she became his wife and bore him a son" (2 Sam 11:27b).

Sounds so right, doesn't it? Everything's going great! A perfectly wonderful new family. *Another well-executed plan, Commander David!* With one exception. See the last words in the verse?

"But the thing David had done displeased the Lord" (2 Sam 11:27c).

Remember that. Because by the time we come to chapter 12 a full year has passed. And as far as David was concerned — he'd gotten off scot-free! He had Bathsheba, and they had their baby! And I'm convinced that David had somehow managed to justify to both himself and those who knew him that his wrong was really quite right.

UNTIL . . . Until a prophet named Nathan came and told David a little story. A story about two men. One who was rich and had a large number of sheep; and one who was poor and had just one little lamb. The rich man had a guest one day, and, instead of choosing from among his many sheep, he took the poor man's *only* sheep and used it for the meal. When David heard that, he flew into a rage! He said, **". . . the man who did this deserves to die!"** (2 Sam 12:5). At that, Nathan got in David's face and said, **"You are the man!"** (2 Sam 12:7).

And like a hot knife through butter, Nathan's words pierced David's heart. And his anger turned to grief. His indignation became remorse. And for the first time in months, he saw himself for what he was: An adulterer, a liar, a thief, even a murderer! David said . . .

> **"Then David said to Nathan, 'I have sinned against the Lord'"** (2 Sam 12:13a).

Psalm 51 reveals David's entire response. It is a song of brokenness. A psalm of absolute surrender. Let there be no doubt: David was repentant. Which is why Nathan said . . .

> **"'The Lord has taken away your sin. You are not going to die'"** (2 Sam 12:13b).

However, David . . .

> **"But because by doing this you have made the enemies of the Lord show utter contempt, the son born to you will die"** (2 Sam 12:14).

> **"Now, therefore, the sword will never depart from your house, because you despised me and took the wife of Uriah the Hittite to be your own"** (2 Sam 12:10).

When you sin, you impose untold grief in your home. God may choose to cover you by His grace, but He has never promised to shield you from the consequences. And not only will you have to endure THE AGONY — but quite often your wife will as well. And your children. And even their children.

God's judgment against David was twofold: *Your baby will die, David. And your family will never know peace. Your home will exist, from this day forward, in a constant state of disarray.*

Sure enough, that's exactly what happened:

> **"This is what the Lord says: 'Out of your own household I am going to bring calamity upon you. Before your very eyes I will take your wives and give them to one who is close to you, and he will lie with your wives in broad daylight'"** (2 Sam 12:11).

Just how close was this person? You want to talk *"close?"* How about one of his own sons? That's right: In chapter 16, after Absalom, David's son, launched his revolution and stormed the palace, he asked his advisors what he should do next.

> "Ahithophel answered, 'Lie with your father's concubines whom he left to take care of the palace. Then all Israel will hear that you have made yourself a stench in your father's nostrils, and the hands of everyone with you will be strengthened.' So they pitched a tent for Absalom on the roof [The very roof where all this mess had begun . . .], and he lay with his father's concubines in the sight of all Israel" (2 Sam 16:21-22).

By the way, that's the first of seven consequences David's family endured: *SEXUAL PROMISCUITY AND UNFAITHFULNESS.*

Consequence #2 was *THE DEATH OF THE INNOCENT.* The Lord had predicted it clearly. The son conceived by Bathsheba was to die.

> "But because by doing this you have made the enemies of the LORD show utter contempt, the son born to you will die" (2 Sam 12:14).

And sure enough . . .

> "After Nathan had gone home, the LORD struck the child that Uriah's wife had borne to David, and he became ill" (2 Sam 12:15).

> "On the seventh day the child died" (2 Sam 12:18a).

Consequence #3 was *INCESTUOUS RAPE.*

> In the course of time, Amnon son of David fell in love with Tamar, the beautiful sister of Absalom son of David" (2 Sam 13:1).

In other words, he fell in love with his half-sister. And it was an inappropriate kind of love. But you see, Amnon had learned from experience that if you want a woman — take her! That's the way dad did it. You see, he was a teenager when Dad took that ill-fated romp on the roof. And he knew full well the scheming, the cover-up, the lying, and the treachery that surrounded that little tête-à-tête. So he faked an illness, and when Tamar came in to bring him some food . . .

> "But when she took it to him to eat, he grabbed her and said, 'Come to bed with me, my sister'" (2 Sam 13:11b).

Steve, are you sure this was a rape? Are you sure Tamar didn't consent?

> "'Don't, my brother!' she said to him. 'Don't force me. Such a thing should not be done in Israel! Don't do this wicked thing.' But he refused to listen to her, and since he was stronger than she, he raped her" (2 Sam 13:12,14).

Are you with me? Because of David's sin, his own son has raped his lovely and affectionate daughter!

Disturbed and distraught, Tamar goes to her other brother — her full-blooded brother, Absalom — who loved her with a healthy kind of love, and she told him what happened. In fact, even before she told him, Absalom seemed to know!

> "Her brother Absalom said to her, 'Has that Amnon, your brother, been with you?'" (2 Sam 13:20a).

It's almost like he suspected it! I tell you, this whole family reeked with a lascivious sensuality!

> "'Be quiet now, my sister; he is your brother. Don't take this thing to heart.' And Tamar lived in her brother Absalom's house, a desolate woman.
> When King David heard all this, he was furious" (2 Sam 13:20b-21).

And that's all well and good — but furious wasn't the biblical response! According to law, Amnon was to be banished! Driven out of the house! Exiled from Israel. But David couldn't bring himself to do that. I wonder if Amnon knew that. I wonder if he had calculated as much before he even raped her. *Aww, Dad will understand.*

> "Absalom never said a word to Amnon, either good or bad; he hated Amnon because he had disgraced his sister Tamar" (2 Sam 13:22).

But more than hate transpired. Absalom simply could not accept the fact that Amnon had played his sister like a fool — and that David let him do it! So, taking matters in his own hands . . .

One Night of Ecstasy, A Whole Lifetime of Agony

> "Absalom ordered his men, 'Listen! When Amnon is in high spirits from drinking wine and I say to you, 'Strike Amnon down,' then kill him. Don't be afraid. Have not I given you this order? Be strong and brave.' So Absalom's men did to Amnon what Absalom had ordered" (2 Sam 13:28-29a).

It was then that Absalom ran away (see verse 37). He couldn't stand the hypocrisy, so he rebelled. Then, after a complicated series of events and a rather lengthy separation, David's military leader, Joab, brought Absalom back to Jerusalem. Evidently, he was convinced that it was time to make restitution. Did restitution happen?

> "But the king said, 'He must go to his own house; he must not see my face.' So Absalom went to his own house and did not see the face of the king" (2 Sam 14:24).

Some welcome home! Unlike the prodigal, who got a ring and a robe and a fatted calf, Absalom was sent to his room. And he seethed with rage. David stubbornly refused to forgive his son — even though, the truth was his son's sin was dad's fault! And for two years they lived liked that.

> "Absalom lived two years in Jerusalem without seeing the king's face" (2 Sam 14:28).

They didn't speak. They never talked. They spent holidays alone. So great was the stubborn anger of David that the gulf between father and son remained intact. And then, when Absalom couldn't stand it any longer — when he realized that he just had to see his dad — he demanded an audience with the king.

> "He came in and bowed down with his face to the ground before the king. And the king kissed Absalom" (2 Sam 14:33b).

Just a peck on the cheek. I don't see here that they talked through their feelings. I don't find any hint that reconciliation was made. All I see is a half-hearted peck on the check. A typical eastern greeting. And that, only because Absalom demanded to see his dad.

That's when the seed of REVOLUTION was planted in Absalom's heart. He determined to take David's throne. And you know what? He almost pulled it off. He won the palace, he won the city, he won the hearts of the people. The only thing that stopped him was a unbelievably freak accident.

> **"He was riding his mule, and as the mule went under the thick branches of a large oak, Absalom's head got caught in the tree. He was left hanging in midair, while the mule he was riding kept on going"** (2 Sam 18:9).

And as he dangled helplessly, Joab found him and plunged three javelins in his heart and killed him.

Now maybe it was just my Sunday School teacher, but when I first learned about Absalom, way back when I was just a squirt, I was taught that Absalom was the "bad guy." I got the impression that he was the black sheep of David's family. He's the one who messed everything up. If it hadn't been for Absalom, David's home would have been like a Norman Rockwell print. And yet the truth is, Absalom wasn't the only one who had problems. Oh, we can build a good case against him. What with the murder and the revolution, not to mention his sleeping with his father's wives — there's no doubt that Absalom was a troubled guy.

But according to chapter 11, it can all be traced back to a father who had blown it. A father who was so caught up in his own lustful ways, he had no spiritual platform from which to confront his sons for their own lustful ways. So a rape went unpunished. And Absalom watched as his sister slumped into depression and despair. She had been violated — and her own father refused to help her.

Dad was a great warrior. He was a powerful king. He was adored by his subjects. But his children knew the truth: *David was a horrible father*. He simply wasn't there when his kids needed him.

I wonder if that's part of the reason David was so distraught? After all, this separation had existed for seven years! And yet, when he received word that Absalom was dead, the Bible says that he . . .

One Night of Ecstasy, A Whole Lifetime of Agony

> "... was shaken. He went up to the room over the gateway and wept. As he went, he said: 'O my son Absalom! My son, my son Absalom! If only I had died instead of you — O Absalom, my son, my son!'" (2 Sam 18:33).

And there he remained for days, weeping for the loss of his son. The whole nation stood dead in its tracks — as the King wept *for* his son. If only he had wept *with* his son. If only he had shown such love while his boy was still alive. As it was, Absalom died never knowing how much his father loved him.

Just as Nathan had predicted, the sword never departed from David's household. That family never again knew joy or peace. *All because of one night of ecstasy.*

HOW TO AVOID THE AGONY

It's sad but true: Such engagements are not uncommon. Even in our day, an affair, a tryst, a romantic encounter is quite the common occurrence. And it happens for a myriad of reasons. In David's case, it was pure, unabashed lust. He saw her, he wanted her. In our day, people have affairs for the same reason. Some fall into the trap because they're trying to prove they've still got it. A middle-aged woman flirts and teases — and ends up sleeping with someone because she's desperately trying to prove she's still attractive. Some men, who used to prove their virility on the ball field, now find that attracting women is what underscores their manhood. Some fall into an affair because they were never taught personal discipline and self-control. Others are self-centered and feel they deserve whatever they think they want. Others are attracted to a stranger because there is unresolved conflict in the home. Still others say that it was unmet needs that did them in. In the search for love and affirmation, in the hope for some meaningful sexual response — they find someone. And in a moment of weakness — BOOM! The deed is done.

I honestly believe that most Christians fall for that very reason. We become disillusioned by our marriage and are convinced that *'someone else can give me what I know I'm not getting from him.'* Ed Young writes:

"A beautiful woman began seeing a marriage counselor. Her walk, her dress, her smile were real attention-getters. She was extremely attractive. 'I'm falling in love with a man in my office,' she said. 'We haven't had sexual relations, but I'm falling in love with him.'

What did the object of her desire look like? *'Oh,' she said, 'If you met him you'd think him the homeliest man you've ever seen. Truthfully, most would say he's ugly. You would never pick him out as someone I'd be attracted to.'*

Why, then? *'Well,' she replied, 'My husband is so cold, so indifferent, so dogmatic, so arrogant. He refuses to communicate with me or try to understand me. I've reached out to him, and done everything I know to do, but he is beyond reach as far as I'm concerned.'*

What about the man at the office? Her eyes lit up immediately. *'He doesn't imagine I'm even interested in him because he is so ordinary. But he's sensitive and warm, he listens to me, encourages me, and is genuinely interested in how I feel. I'm afraid of what I'm flirting with. I know it is sin, but I'm just so hungry for understanding and kindness and communication.'"*

Young adds: "How sad that a wife's need for affection is met by a near stranger when it should be the habit of her husband to do so. How equally sad when a man's need for sexual fulfillment is met outside the ideal atmosphere of marriage because it is not the habit of his wife to give herself to him."[1]

He's right. IT **IS** SAD. But it happens nonetheless. And if it's happened to you — the truth is, you *can* recover. You can be forgiven. You won't escape the consequences of your actions, but you can be covered by God's grace. However, the very best advice I can give you — in fact, the whole meat and purpose of this chapter is this:

*IF YOU **HAVEN'T** FALLEN, **DON'T!***

If you are dancing right now on the edge of compromise — if you are beginning to entertain thoughts of YES! — before you take one step further, before you allow yourself one more look, before you think one more thought — STOP! Give it up! Strangle the life from that fantasy! Take that alien thought into captivity and strike it down! For if you don't, it's just a matter of time before you fall.

One Night of Ecstasy, A Whole Lifetime of Agony

And if your mind is racing right now, trying to figure out who in the world I'm writing to — who in your church or small group would think of doing such a thing (because good Christians don't think such thoughts) then, my friend, you're in worse shape than the rest of us. I find it true without exception: **IF YOU WANT TO KEEP FROM FALLING, YOU MUST DILIGENTLY REAFFIRM YOUR VULNERABILITY.**

The Bible says, **"Take heed when you think you stand, lest you fall"** (1 Cor 10:12). David was a man after God's own heart. A righteous worship leader. A spiritual defender of the truth. But he still blew it. And so can you. And if you think otherwise, you are a fool.

I know I'm capable of such compromise. And because I don't trust myself, I try to build tall, protective hedges in my life. For one, I never have lunch alone with another woman. I just never do that. I never ride in a car alone with another woman. When I counsel, I counsel during office hours and with a secretary just outside my door. And whenever possible, when I'm traveling, someone is with me — so there is never an open door for inappropriate behavior. When I check into a hotel, I ask the clerk to disconnect all access to Spectravision. When I rent a movie, it's a movie I could watch with my children.

Now you might hear that and think, *"Wyatt, you are a prude!"* In fact, I've had several people tell me that. And that's OK. The way I see it, I have very little to gain by tempting fate — and a whole lot to lose. I don't bet on the golf course, and I'm not going to bet with my marriage either.

I love the words of Mark Twain: *"There are several good protections against temptations, but the surest is cowardice."* I like that. And I practice cowardice with great regularity.

There's something else you need to do: You must also **CONTINUALLY REMIND YOURSELF THAT SIN'S PENALTIES FAR OUTWEIGH SIN'S PLEASURE.** That would be David's testimony, I assure you.

He found the promise of Scripture to be true: **"Do not be** deceived: God cannot be mocked. A man reaps what he sows" (Gal 6:7).

Solomon adds:

> **"Can a man scoop fire into his lap without his clothes being burned? Can a man walk on hot coals without his feet being scorched? So is he who sleeps with another man's wife; no one who touches her will go unpunished"** (Prov 6:27-29).

Listen friend: The next time you're tempted toward adultery — pull out this chapter. Take another look at Galatians 6:7-8. Review the conclusion that Solomon made. Then rehearse the lifelong agony David endured for one fleeting moment of pleasure.

Would he say it was worth it?

What do you think? Listen: *The price sin demands is far greater than the pleasure sin delivers. So if you haven't fallen yet, DON'T! It's not worth it.*

Now maybe this message is too late for you. Maybe you've already blown it. If so, my counsel to you is this:

IF YOU HAVE FALLEN . . . STOP!

The very fact that you are reading these words is a testimony not to God's approval, but to His grace. He longs for you to repent and seek His healing. But don't play fast and loose with God's mercy. Don't take advantage of His kindness. Because the Bible says that the time will come when God will **"hand you over"** to do whatever you want to do. So stop! Now! And before you take another breath, initiate these three steps:

#1: CONFESS YOUR FAULT.

Go first to the Lord and then to those you have offended and deal honestly with the blame. Your blame. I don't care what she did to drive you to this. This is your stage. This is your curtain call.

A minister was finishing a message on adultery and he said, *"And so, we've got to stop this sin of adultery and I pray right now that every person that's guilty of the sin of adultery, that right this moment their tongue would stick to the woof a dier mouts!"*

Deal with your own life, buster. Trust me, that's a full-time job. You worry about you; let God worry about her life.

#2: CONTACT GOD'S GRACE.

Come before him in the spirit of 1 John 1:9 and confess to him your sin and claim His mercy and His grace. And He will give it. That doesn't mean you won't face the music. His perfect consequences may still come. But you still have to come clean.

#3: COMMUNICATE WITH YOUR MATE.

Tell her the truth. And then begin the long, difficult journey toward healing. Give it time. You didn't get in this mess overnight, and it won't heal overnight.

Make no mistake: Adultery isn't healthy — it's sick. It doesn't prove you're independent and strong — it's a bold declaration that you are a very weak person. It isn't an affair — it's adultery. It isn't a relationship — it's wrong. A MILLION DOLLARS OR NOT — IT'S NOT WORTH IT. So give it up.

A FINAL WORD . . . TO THE OFFENDED

If you have been the victim of an unfaithful partner, I want you to know that adultery isn't the end of the world. Recovery is possible. So before you do something rash, take some time to catch your breath. Spend some time asking God for wisdom and for peace.

And remember this: As violated as you may feel — the truth is, you have some freight to pay in this too. After twenty years in the ministry, I have yet to meet the infamous *"innocent party."* I don't think such a person exists. Everyone makes mistakes in their marriage, and you're no exception. Adultery doesn't "just happen." So don't go off half-cocked and shoot somebody. Don't put sugar in her gas tank or drive nails in his tires. And don't go out and find some cute thing for yourself either. Instead, why not invest that same energy in seeking out ways the two of you can rebuild?

In his book, *The Myth of the Greener Grass*, J. Allan Petersen writes: *"The affair is a sign of a need for help, an attempt to compensate for deficiencies . . . a warning that someone is suffering."*

I know: The last thing you want to hear is that the one who hurt you is hurting too. You're suffering! And no, perhaps no other person will ever fully understand your pain, but God does. And He longs to be your refuge and your strength.

In fact, there's a great verse in Genesis 41:52 that says: **"God has made me fruitful in the land of my suffering."** He can do that in your life too. He can totally reconstruct your marriage. You may need counseling, you may need a long time for recovery. But if you're willing, and if your mate is willing — in time, God can give you a new beginning. He can make you fruitful in the land of your suffering.

NOTES

[1] Ed Young, *Romancing the Home* (Nashville: Broadman & Holman Publishers, 1993), pp. 112-113.

CHAPTER FIVE

Lust Is a Many Splintered Thing
JUDGES 13–16

You cannot imagine my delight recently when I learned that 29-year-old power forward, A.C. Green, one of the stars during the championship days of the Los Angeles Lakers basketball team and now a member of the Phoenix Suns organization, is still a virgin. Despite the fact that young females line the sidewalks of every NBA city where he plays — essentially throwing themselves at him — A.C. has refused to succumb to the pressure. He offers two reasons for that amazing fact. First, because he loves God. Second, because he's not yet married and wants to save himself as a gift to his future wife. My one-word reaction? Wow! *WHAT A CONTRAST TO HIS FORMER TEAMMATE.*

You need to know that I have always been a fan of Magic Johnson. Ever since that miraculous NCAA championship game in 1979, I have followed his career with amazement. From the day he put on the purple and gold I became a slobbering, die-hard Lakers fan. And I was terribly saddened when I learned, as you did, that he was tested HIV positive. I don't wish that disease on anyone. And yes, like so many others, I was amazed at his courageous and public admission. It took guts to say what he said.

But don't forget what he said. He said that he had acquired

the virus through *"heterosexual activity."* Let's cut to the chase, shall we? That means he slept around. In fact, he was almost bragging when he told *Sports Illustrated:*

> *I am certain that I was infected by having unprotected sex with a woman who has the virus. The problem is that I can't pinpoint the time, the place or the woman. It's a matter of numbers. Before I was married, I truly lived the bachelor's life . . . as I traveled around NBA cities, I was never at a loss for female companionships . . . I confess that after I arrived in L. A., in 1979, I did my best to accommodate as many women as I could — most of them through unprotected sex.*[1]

Will someone please explain to me: *"Why all the praise for Magic and virtual silence for A.C.?"* Why have we heaped lavish accolades on the slackish lifestyle of a pervert, but then shrug our shoulders at the admirable self-control of Mr. Green? And, if the truth were known, secretly wonder whether the guy even *likes* girls?

Magic Johnson is no hero. I agree with Walt Wangerin: *"A randy sexuality doth not a hero make."* Really! It's easy to let your glands rule your life. That's no cause for public admiration! Anybody can pull that off! I love the response Ann Landers gave to the following letter:

> *Dear Ann,*
> *I have been sleeping with three women for several months. Until a few days ago, none of them knew that the others existed and things were going fine. By chance, two of them met each other, compared notes, and found me out. Now they are furious with me. What am I going to do?*
> *P. S. Please don't give me any of your moral junk.*
> *Signed,*
> *Trapped.*

Landers replied:

> *Dear Trapped,*
> *The one major thing that separates the human race from animals is a God-given sense of morality. Since you don't have a sense of morality, I strongly suggest you consult a veterinarian.*[2]

Lust Is a Many Splintered Thing

Good response, Ann. Yet sadly, *Trapped* is not alone. As I survey our culture, I find an entire society literally oozing with sensuality. The atmosphere of life in the 1990s is sexually charged. We're infatuated with fine, firmly toned bodies. We're drowning in a sea of sexually suggestive propaganda. Walk into any convenience store in America and it hits you right in the face. Walk through the mall and you have to deal with it. Turn on the tube and you're instantly bombarded by ad after ad loaded with double entendre and suggestive innuendo. Just consider for a moment the billboards, the magazine covers, the posters, the VCR tapes, the movie channels. Lust, indeed, has become our national pastime.

*So what's the big deal, Steve? Sex is just fun and games. After all we are sexual creatures and we do have all these sexual drives: What's wrong with gratifying them? You know, if it feels good, do it! That's **my** motto.* And therein lies the problem.

For in our hapless, unbridled pursuit of a good time, we have left in our wake untold havoc and destruction. Violent sex crimes are at an all-time high. Date rapes on college campuses have become commonplace. Extramarital affairs are excused, even justified. Teenage pregnancies are old news — and a quick trip to the big city, a couple of hundred dollars, and a medical murder can put the whole ugly mess back in the closet. AIDS continues to claim the lives of homosexual offenders. Cases of syphilis and gonorrhea have tripled in less than three years. And with the percentage of young Americans becoming sexually active at record-setting early ages — for example, one-fourth of all fifteen-year old girls are sexually active — the problems are certain to proliferate.

And make no mistake, this cultural mindset is impacting *your* home, too. I talked with a mom sometime ago who told me that a neighbor boy, a kindergartner, walked up to her daughter, called her name and said, *"I think you're sexy. Take off your shirt and let me kiss you."*

Now some may find that cute, but after 20 years of cleaning up the debris of wholesale sexual freedom, after 20 years of trying to help mend the horrible wounds of incest, after 20 years of trying to rebuild families ripped apart by some meaningless affair, after 20 years of dealing with men hooked on pornography, after 20 years of giving counsel to those hopelessly trapped in homosexuality, after 20 years of hearing of one minister after another who has sacrificed his family, his church, and his ministry on the altar of his own libido — I find very little about that that is cute.

Now just so you know I'm not some fuddy-duddy, let me assure you, I enjoy sex. And our God is not the great killjoy when it comes to sex, either. You need to know that. God created sex, not Hugh Hefner. And when He did, He said, **"It is VERY good."** Everything else God made — the trees, the birds, the elephants, the orangutans were just **"good."** But the male-female relationship, complete with sexual drives and capacities for reproduction, God said, **"It is VERY good."** And Adam wholeheartedly agreed! Remember how he reacted when he woke up from his little nap, and there **"she"** was!? Up till that time, Adam had only had animals for companions. And animals are OK as pets, but they're the pits when it comes to lifelong partnering. So when Adam saw Eve, he said, ***"WOW! This is bone of my bones and flesh of my flesh! You done good, God!"***

Listen, sex is for our pleasure, not just procreation. Sex is a beautiful gift from God. It is neither dirty, rotten, nor ugly. God created sex, and He only creates GOOD THINGS.

The problem is, people are taking God's good gift and they're prostituting it. They're expressing their sexuality in ways and in relationships God never intended and refuses to bless.

Now they do what they do in an honest search for intimacy, but they are inevitably trapped by the very thing they think will set them free. Why? Because sex apart from God's plan promises big, but delivers little. Instead of ecstasy, most people find casual sex to be fraught with emptiness. Instead of fulfillment, sex sin leads to frustration.

Lust Is a Many Splintered Thing

Now understand, it's not the sex that's bad, but the way the sex is handled — that's what's bad. And things have become so bad in our day, that *Playboy* magazine, once on the leading edge of sexual propaganda, has become passé. Its readership has plummeted, Playboy Clubs are now defunct, and the Chicago Playboy mansion is now an art school. WHY?

> *"In a sense,"* said Playboy publicity chief Dennis Salyers, *"we worked ourselves out of a job. At one time, we were on the leading edge of sexual change in this country. Nowadays, nobody here would want to be on the leading edge of sexual change because it would mean doing it with kangaroos or something."*[23]

There you have it — not from the lips of a preacher, but from one of the original purveyors of sexual freedom. From the very voice that led us down this primrose path: *"The leading edge of sexual change"* in America is *"doing it with kangaroos . . ."*

CALL THE VET, ANN! Because America is literally brimming with perverted lust. The sin that hisses. L-u-s-s-s-s-t. The sin that took God's beautiful gift and made it ugly.

Now don't get me wrong — lust, and the havoc it creates, is hardly new. Case in point? Samson, the dauntless champion of Israel!

You remember Samson. Certainly every male who went to Sunday School remembers Samson. Samson, the man who killed lions and slayed the thousands. Samson, the infamous strong man. What little boy hasn't dreamed of being like Samson? Rippling biceps, washboard stomach, legs as big as tree trunks. Samson, my hero.

Yet despite his obvious physical prowess, mommies and daddies have never taken to his name. There aren't many kiddos running around these days answering to Samson. *Why?* Because the strong man of Israel was held hostage by his own lust, that's why. And his life came to a tragic end because of it.

RAISED BY SPIRITUAL PARENTS

Now Samson's life didn't start out that way. The fact is, Samson was raised by godly, spiritual parents. I mention that because it's easy to assume that a man as reprobate as Samson had to have been born that way. Maybe it was a rotten environment — that's what did him in. Or maybe he had a daddy who abused him — that's why he liked to beat up on people. Or maybe the family had no scruples in their financial dealings, and Samson learned from his earliest days how to pander to his own fleshly, carnal desires. Interesting analyses to be sure, but entirely false.

Judges 13 tells the story of a godly man and woman who for years had yearned for a child, but the woman's womb was barren. Until one day, **"the angel of the LORD appeared"** and announced the birth of Samson. He said:

"... you will conceive and give birth to a son" (Judg 13:5a).

But not just any kind of son. This baby is going to be a very special young man.

"No razor may be used on his head, because the boy is to be a Nazirite, set apart to God from birth..." (Judg 13:5b).

According to Numbers 6, a Nazirite was one who was wholly devoted to God by a vow that he took of his own free will. Three characteristics marked the Nazirite. He never cut his hair, he maintained a rigorous diet, and he never touched anything that was dead. Now understand, Samson took that vow of his own accord, but God revealed from the womb that he would do so. Keep reading, because even his occupation is prophesied.

"... and he will begin the deliverance of Israel from the hands of the Philistines" (Judg 13:5c).

Samson would begin the process of Israel's redemption from their age-old nemesis — Philistia. And sure enough ...

"The woman gave birth to a boy and named him Samson. He grew and the LORD blessed him" (Judg 13:24).

By the way, I have a word for godly parents whose children have gone bad. You need to know, mom and dad, that you can do everything right for your son, and that son can still can go wrong. You can raise your daughter in an atmosphere of reverence and purity — but it's no guarantee that when she's on her own, that she will walk with God. I wish there was such a guarantee, but there is not. I have witnessed firsthand the ache in the heart of a spiritual parent for the rebellion of her carnal child. It's a shame, a deep heartache that simply cannot be described.

Here's Samson: The recipient of a home life that was right and true. And yet, because of his own free will, because he himself chose to yield — Samson became a blind clown, forced to wallow in the dung of a Philistine dungeon. He knew better. He was raised right. But he had a weakness in his flesh — he entertained lust in his heart. He allowed his sensual passion to rule him.

RULED BY SENSUAL PASSIONS

By the time we come to chapter 14, Samson is now a young man.

"Samson went down to Timnah and saw there a young Philistine woman" (Judg 14:1).

Note that: He saw her. There's no indication that he dated her. Or even talked to her until later (v. 7). He just **"saw"** her.

"When he returned, he said to his father and mother, 'I have seen a Philistine woman in Timnah . . .'" (Judg 14:2a).

Isn't that wild? The first recorded words from Samson's mouth are, *"I saw a woman!"* Does that tell you where this man was coming from? And without even the slightest concern for her heathen upbringing, caring little for her values or her intellect or even her basic personality, he said to his parents, *"I have seen a Philistine woman in Timnah . . .*

" . . . get her for me as my wife" (Judg 14:2b).

Now guys, our wives have the toughest time understanding that. They can't imagine how it is that a man can become fascinated with a picture in a magazine. Or a model on TV. Or a stranger in the mall. But we understand . . . don't we?

Now mom and dad tried desperately to talk him out of this.

> **"His father and mother replied, 'Isn't there an acceptable woman among your relatives or among all our people? Must you go to the uncircumcised Philistines to get a wife?' But Samson said to his father, 'Get her for me. She's the right one for me'"** (Judg 14:3).

It literally reads: *"She looks good to me!"* That's all that matters, Dad. She's a looker. A babe. A fox. What can I say? So with that, Samson and his parents head to Timnah to make the necessary arrangements. Verse 4 reveals that God intended to use this circumstance, but Samson wasn't thinking of God.

> **"Samson went down to Timnah together with his father and mother. As they approached the vineyards of Timnah, suddenly a young lion came roaring toward him. The Spirit of the LORD came upon him in power so that he tore the lion apart with his bare hands as he might have torn a young goat. But he told neither his father nor his mother what he had done. Then he went down and talked with the woman, and he liked her"** (Judg 14:5-7).

The New American Standard underscores it again, saying, **"She looked good to Samson."** I want you to see that Scripture is building a case: Samson was a man driven by his lust. And the first of Five Fatal Flaws can be seen in the verse we just read:

Fatal Flaw #1: SAMSON WAS MORE INTRIGUED BY HOW THE WOMAN LOOKED THAN BY WHAT THE WOMAN WAS LIKE.

Ruled by his passions, Samson checked out her bod, and was so thoroughly impressed — he just had to have her. The poor girl isn't even named for us! Because her name wasn't the point; her body was the point.

I wonder, what do you notice first when you're with someone of the opposite sex? What is it that occupies your attention when you're on a date? What is it about a person that attracts you to them?

At a recent Praise Gathering my wife and I attended, one of the younger (and I might add quite handsome) members of the Gaither Vocal Band walked right by the place where Vanessa and I were sitting. And he was dressed good, and he even smelled good! Now please understand, my wife is a paragon of purity. She is the most morally upright person I know. But this was one good-looking dude! And so, out of the corner of my eye, I watched her follow him around the corner and right out of the room. Her neck turned so far, I thought she'd broken the thing! I leaned over and said, *"Caught ya!"* She turned about 73 shades of crimson, punched me in the ribs and said, *"Only because I'm not as practiced at it as you are!"* Thwapp! Right in the heart. Because she's right. My eyes are a constant battleground.

And if you don't admit the same, you are a liar. Which is why Jesus suggested that you and I may want to just pluck those dudes out! Because there is a direct connection between lust and how we use our eyes.

All the way back in Genesis, Eve decided to eat the apple simply because she **"saw that the tree was good for food and that it was a delight to the eyes"** (Gen 3:6).

It was the eyes that got David into trouble, too. Understand, David didn't sin because he happened to notice Bathsheba bathing on her roof one day. He'd been camping on that roof.

I agree with Martin Luther: *"One cannot keep a bird from landing on one's head, but one can keep him from building a nest there."* Looking is not lusting. You can't help but look when a good looking hunk walks by. But there's a line that is crossed when looking becomes lusting — and you know what that line is. David had crossed it. David's problem is not that he looked, but that he had been staring. And not just staring, he had been gawking! Till finally, having rehearsed the act dozens of times in his heart, he actually did the deed.

Job is another who realized the power of the eye. That's why he said in **Job 31**, **"I have made a covenant with my eyes, not to look with lust upon a woman"** (Job 31:1).

Frankly, I doubt that anyone has ever blown it physically without first having fallen victim to lust through their eyes. But remember, the eyes only reflect the condition of the heart. You look with lust upon another person, and it simply reveals the decadence that is already within you.

And the point is: if it's true that your eyes look at whatever your heart is focused on — put a governor on your heart! Before you look, stop the thoughts! For if you allow your eyes to feast on the physical attributes of someone who is not your mate — you are a goner. It's just a matter of time before you fall.

Look at how it happened in Samson's life:

> **"Some time later, when he went back to marry her, he turned aside to look at the lion's carcass. In it was a swarm of bees and some honey, which he scooped out with his hands and ate as he went along"** (Judg 14:8-9a).

By the way, he did that in direct violation of his Nazarite vow.

> **"When he rejoined his parents, he gave them some, and they too ate it. But he did not tell them that he had taken the honey from the lion's carcass. Now his father went down to see the woman. And Samson made a feast there, as was customary for bridegrooms. When he appeared, he was given thirty companions"** (Judg 14:9b-11).

They were to serve as his bridegrooms. And as they waited for the feast to begin, Samson said . . .

> **"'Let me tell you a riddle,' Samson said to them. 'If you can give me the answer within the seven days of the feast, I will give you thirty linen garments and thirty sets of clothes. If you can't tell me the answer, you must give me thirty linen garments and thirty sets of clothes.' 'Tell us your riddle,' they said. 'Let's hear it.' He replied, 'Out of the eater, something to eat; out of the strong, something sweet.' For three days they could not give the answer"** (Judg 14:12-14).

Of course not. Only Samson knew the story.

Lust Is a Many Splintered Thing

> "On the fourth day, they said to Samson's wife, 'Coax your husband [The word **"coax"** means "entice, persuade, seduce him . . ."] into explaining the riddle for us, or we will burn you and your father's household to death. Did you invite us here to rob us?'
>
> "Then Samson's wife threw herself on him, sobbing, 'You hate me! You don't really love me. You've given my people a riddle, but you haven't told me the answer.' 'I haven't even explained it to my father or mother,' he replied, 'so why should I explain it to you?'
>
> "She cried the whole seven days of the feast" (Judg 14:15-17a).

She knew the weakness of this man. He was into pleasure. And seven days of tears was no pleasure! Why, as lustful as he was, he probably couldn't even handle one evening's worth of such a headache!

> "So on the seventh day he finally told her, because she continued to press him. She in turn explained the riddle to her people. Before sunset on the seventh day the men of the town said to him, 'What is sweeter than honey? What is stronger than a lion?' Samson said to them, 'If you had not plowed with my heifer, you would not have solved my riddle'" (Judg 14:17b-18).

Guys, I don't recommend that you use that phrase, OK? Don't go home and call your honey a heifer. It wouldn't be prudent . . . at this or any other juncture.

> Then the Spirit of the LORD came upon him in power. He went down to Ashkelon, struck down thirty of their men, stripped them of their belongings and gave their clothes to those who had explained the riddle. Burning with anger, he went up to his father's house. And Samson's wife was given to the friend who had attended him at his wedding" (Judg 14:19-20).

The whole marriage was called off!

Now evidently, in the backwash of this moral failure, Samson did a mid-course correction. According to **Judges 15:20, "Samson judged Israel for twenty years."** There is no hint of sensuality or lust. No suggestion that he battled with his aggressive, angry spirit. I take it that he lived the straight life for several years. He judged the people with moral integrity and purity. Until . . .

"One day Samson went to Gaza, where he saw a prostitute. [There are those eyes again . . .] **He went in to spend the night with her"** (Judg 16:1).

After a few years of doing it right — one sniff of perfume, one glance at a shapely young frame — and Samson slides right down the tubes! Again, the woman isn't even named! Because he didn't fall for a woman, he fell for a body.

Which brings us to *Fatal Flaw #2: SAMSON FELL BECAUSE HE ASSUMED THAT A BATTLE ONCE FOUGHT WAS A BATTLE FOREVER WON.*

Don't you believe it, friend. The battle is never really over. So don't ever let your guard down. Not even for a minute.

Frederick Buechner writes:

"Lust is the ape that gibbers in our loins; tame him, as we will by day, he rages all the wilder in our dreams by night. Just when we think we're safe from him, he raises up his ugly head and smirks. And there's no river in the world flows cold and strong enough to strike him down. Almighty God, why dost Thou deck men out with such a loathesome toy?"[4]

Why indeed? My friend, if you have a bent toward lust, if you find strange delight in things carnal and fleshly, you will never know a day when that delight will die. NEVER.

When I made similar comments at the church where I serve, a distinguished Christian gentleman approached me after the service and said, *"Steve, what you said this morning is true. I am 71 years old. I have two children and five grandchildren. And there's not a day in my life that I don't battle with my lust."*

That's why, like it or not, you must always keep your guard up. And don't ever assume that you're too old, or too mature, or too godly to blow it. A battle once fought — will be fought again. I guarantee it.

Once the slide began, not even powerful Samson was strong enough to stop it.

"Some time later, he fell in love with a woman in the Valley of Sorek whose name was Delilah" (Judg 16:4).

Lust Is a Many Splintered Thing

Finally! A woman with a name! But where did he find this woman? In Sorek, a place known for its sensuality. A place Alfred Edersheim calls, *"the place of the choice red grape."*[25] It was the Vegas of the ancient world. A place for tramps and floozies. A place of carnality and compromise. Now time out! What's Samson supposed to be doing with his life? He's supposed to be delivering Israel! Instead, he's out cruising for babes.

Which brings us to ***Fatal Flaw #3:*** *SAMSON BLEW IT BECAUSE HE RAN WITH THE WRONG CROWD.*

First, there were the thirty Philistines back at the feast exchanging silly riddles. And now, the gang in Sorek! *What's he doing hanging around places like that?* Listen friend, if you have a problem with lust, don't hang around the video store. If you have a problem with greed, don't play the lottery. If you've battled your whole life with alcohol, don't drink Cokes at the corner bar.

And yet, here's Samson, cruising Sorek — of all places — and he finds a real babe in Delilah. Some of his so-called buddies find out about this fling, so . . .

> **"The rulers of the Philistines went to her and said, 'See if you can lure him** [. . . entice him, seduce him . . .] **into showing you the secret of his great strength and how we can overpower him so we may tie him up and subdue him. Each one of us will give you eleven hundred shekels of silver"** (Judg 16:5).

Now that was no small piece of change, friend. So she agrees. And knowing all too well his obvious weakness, Delilah played Samson like a 5-string banjo.

> **"So Delilah said to Samson, 'Tell me the secret of your great strength and how you can be tied up and subdued'"** (Judg 16:6).

Which tells you that Samson was not a very smart guy. At least not when his lust was inflamed. Which is generally the case, I might add. When lust is inflamed, wisdom shuts down. Really! Consider Samson. Delilah has just told him exactly what the Philistines want to do to him! And he still decides to play along!

Behind the Tent Flaps

I picture her getting all dolled up, putting on some exotic see-through veils discreetly hiding just enough to really grab his interest, and then she snuggles up beside him and says, *"Tell me your secret, Sammy!"*

Sure enough, Samson, intrigued by the allurement of the moment, decides to play along.

> "Samson answered her, 'If anyone ties me with seven fresh thongs that have not been dried, I'll become as weak as any other man.' Then the rulers of the Philistines brought her seven fresh thongs that had not been dried, and she tied him with them. With men hidden in the room, she called to him, 'Samson, the Philistines are upon you!' But he snapped the thongs as easily as a piece of string snaps when it comes close to a flame. So the secret of his strength was not discovered" (Judg 16:7-9).

Notice Delilah's response . . .

> "'You have made a fool of me; you lied to me. Come now, tell me how you can be tied.' He said, 'If anyone ties me securely with new ropes that have never been used, I'll become as weak as any other man'" (Judg 16:10-11).

This man never seemed to get it, did he? He's supposed to be delivering people. That's the whole reason why he was born. Yet, if it's not riddles, it's cruising. If it's not cruising, it's a game of sexual tease.

> "So Delilah took new ropes and tied him with them. Then, with men hidden in the room, she called to him, 'Samson, the Philistines are upon you!' But he snapped the ropes off his arms as if they were threads.
>
> Delilah then said to Samson, 'Until now, you have been making a fool of me and lying to me. Tell me how you can be tied.' He replied, 'If you weave the seven braids of my head into the fabric [on the loom] and tighten it with the pin, I'll become as weak as any other man'" (Judg 16:12-13a).

Time out! You've gone too far, Samson. You're much too close to the fire!

By the way, that's ***Fatal Flaw #4:*** *SAMSON IS TOYING WITH THE SACRED.*

In order to keep the thrill going, in order to get the same high as he got the last time — Samson comes closer and closer to the heart of the truth.

"So while he was sleeping, Delilah took the seven braids of his head, wove them into the fabric and tightened it with the pin. Again she called to him, 'Samson, the Philistines are upon you!' He awoke from his sleep and pulled up the pin and the loom, with the fabric" (Judg 16:13b-14).

And now, he's gone too far to get out. Delilah hasn't played her trump card — but it's coming now.

"Then she said to him, 'How can you say, "I love you," when you won't confide in me? [*What husband hasn't heard that line? You won't let me into your life. You never tell me what you're thinking! How can you say, 'I love you?'*] **This is the third time you have made a fool of me and haven't told me the secret of your great strength.'" With such nagging she prodded him day after day until he was tired to death"** (Judg 16:15-16).

The Hebrew word means, *"Utterly worn out."* Can you imagine? Some of you can. Incessant nagging day in and day out. What did Samson do? Well, what would *you* do?

". . . he told her everything" (Judg 16:17a).

That's *Fatal Flaw #5. HE TOLD HER "EVERYTHING" THAT WAS IN HIS HEART.*

Key word? **"Everything."** He unloaded every secret he had. Now in the story of Samson, "everything" had to do with his hair. In your marriage it may be the secret disappointment of your choice. It may be that you're unsatisfied with your wife's sexual performance. Or maybe your **"everything"** is a husband who doesn't love you, who refuses to meet your emotional needs. And yet, the minute you decide to tell **"everything,"** it's over.

You parade the heartache of your life before someone other than your mate — and you've put your marriage on the blocks. *Do you understand that there are intimacies that should never be shared? That there are realities that should never be discussed? Especially with a member of the opposite sex?* There are "secret things" that ought to remain a secret. And ought to be discussed between you and God alone. It's through prayer and meditation that God ministers to such heartaches. And they belong to Him, Moses said (see Deuteronomy 29:29), and not to any other.

But Samson told it all. He said:

> "'No razor has ever been used on my head,' he said, 'because I have been a Nazirite set apart to God since birth. If my head were shaved, my strength would leave me, and I would become as weak as any other man'" (Judg 16:17).

Delilah, perceiving that Samson had finally come clean, sprang into action.

> "When Delilah saw that he had told her everything, she sent word to the rulers of the Philistines, 'Come back once more; he has told me everything.' So the rulers of the Philistines returned with the silver in their hands. Having put him to sleep on her lap, she called a man to shave off the seven braids of his hair, and so began to subdue him. And his strength left him. Then she called, 'Samson, the Philistines are upon you!' He awoke from his sleep and thought, 'I'll go out as before and shake myself free.' But he did not know that the LORD had left him" (Judg 16:18-20).

Did you know that you can be so preoccupied with lustful plans and presumptuous acts of sin that you don't even realize it when God leaves?

> "Then the Philistines seized him, gouged out his eyes and took him down to Gaza. Binding him with bronze shackles, they set him to grinding in the prison" (Judg 16:21).

Can you believe it? Israel's great white hope! The defender of God's people! The deliverer of Israel! Now imprisoned and blind. Chained to a mill, forced to walk in the excrement of his fellow prisoners.

I know this is straight-up stuff. And I'm giving it to you unfiltered because with great regularity I encounter a lot of people — even good people! — who are dancing on the edge of disaster. And you think you can handle it! You may even think you're getting away with it!

Lust Is a Many Splintered Thing

If that's where you are right now — you are a fool. Listen to me: Not even Samson could handle it. Even the strong man of Dan proved weak. And the very people he came to conquer, conquered him. The very eyes that had brought him so much pleasure were gouged out, never to wander again. The Champion of Israel had become a clown.

HOW TO AVOID SAMSON'S SLIDE

One man has said that lust is a *"short pleasure, bought with long pain, a honeyed poison, a gulf of shame."*[26] Calvin Miller compares lust to a *"cannibal committing suicide by nibbling on himself."* Great imagery.

Maybe you're wondering: *How do I conquer this thing? I don't want to end up like Samson. I don't want to become a clown. How can I find victory?* I want to share with you **THREE PRACTICAL STEPS** that you can take. And if you really want to conquer this monster, these steps are a great place to start.

Step #1: *You Must Reject Any And All Rationalizations.*

You've got to stop making excuses for yourself. You've got to stop justifying your sin. You must stop coming up with 38 reasons why you do what you do. If will ever know victory, you've got to put all those excuses aside and admit your need.

We're all masters in the art of self-justification, aren't we? Let me give you just a partial list of some of the excuses I've heard:

- *"Steve, I'm homosexual, but I can't help it; I was born that way!"* (Oh no you weren't.)
- *"Steve, my wife doesn't love me like she should. She's a cold fish. She refuses to meet my needs."*
- *"Steve, how can I know we're compatible if we don't have sex before we get married?"*
- *"Steve, I'm so lonely. Surely God will understand."*
- *"Steve, I find that pornography actually **helps** our sex life. A good porno tape is just the thing to put the zing back into our sex life."* (Really?)

Listen, the next time you catch yourself buying into the hedonistic, pleasure-seeking, lust-filled priorities of our world — throw it down! Toss it out! Reject it! Refuse to excuse your sin! Until you do, you will *never*, **never**! know victory.

A number of years ago I received an unsolicited note from a dear Christian woman. A woman who, by her own admission, spent much of her life entangled in a web of unholy lust. I was preparing to preach on a similar theme as this, and she wrote me saying,

"I read ahead and knew what you were going to talk about on Sunday, and I knew you'd research it very well. But I've been there, and I thought maybe some of my thoughts could help you."

Across the page were these four words: **"What I have Learned."** Those words have blood all over them, folks. She's been there. She knows of what she speaks. She wrote,

"Sex without love is pleasurable (for the moment). But the consequences are long-term. You never fully recover. Sex with love, but without commitment, eventually leads to frustration because you begin to question why there can't be more to the relationship. As a result, insecurity dominates. Sex outside of marriage results in a distrust by others and yourself— and that sense of distrust seems impossible to forget. Sex apart from God's plan is disobedience. And disobedience to God negatively affects my relationship to the only One who consistently and unconditionally loves me!"

My heart goes out to this woman. You see, she understands the message of Samson. She knows too well that the fun and games are followed, inevitably, by imprisonment and even death.

Step #1 is clear: Do not be deceived. To all of the persuasions that are used against you — strike them down! Stop excusing your behavior. Until you do, you'll never rise above.

Step #2: *You Must Remove Yourself From The Scene.*

Paul told the Corinthians, **"You must flee!"** Except that it's written in the present imperative, so it carries the idea of a continual, ongoing action. *"Flee sexual immorality! And keep fleeing! And if it continues to hound you, keep on fleeing until the moment of danger is past!"*

That's what Joseph did. When Potiphar's wife tried to seduce him, not once, but over and over again — day after day after day — he removed himself from her. And even when she arranged for an empty house and displayed herself in all her glory — even then, Joseph, rather than trying to explain, rather than trying to convince her it wasn't right — turned tail and ran!

Do you know why that's such a great plan? Because you can't negotiate with lust. You can't reason with sensuality. And listen, lust should never be considered a spiritual challenge to be met, but rather a spiritual trap to be escaped. The wisest, most logical response when lust threatens to get the upper hand is to get out!

Now you'll only take that advice if you are convinced that lust is dangerous and to be avoided at all costs. Otherwise, you'll finagle some way to rationalize why your situation is different. But if you know in your heart that you're playing with fire — and that one of these days you're gonna get burned — then cut out of your life anything or anyone that threatens to take you down!

That's what Jesus said. **"If your right eye causes you to sin, gouge it out. It is better for you to lose one part of your body than for your whole body to be thrown into hell"** (Matt 5:29). Tough words, but true.

So what do you need to cut out of **your** life? Perhaps its a meaningful relationship that has gotten out of hand. Maybe it's your reading material, perhaps your VCR.

More than anything else, some of you need to simply **"flee"** your present playgrounds and playmates. You need a new environment, and you need new friends. And it's amazing! If you will do that, if you will do away with the magazines and the books and films and the jokes and the flirtatious relationships — if you will cut them out — and flee from them — you can begin to starve the life from those overactive fantasies, from the stranglehold that lust has on you. And those seemingly uncontrollable thoughts? In time, they will begin to just melt away.

Step #3: *You Must Reconnect With God.*

Harold Myra puts it best in a little poem-prayer entitled, *"Why the Jet-Sex Engine?"* He writes:

> *"Thanks, Lord, thanks for our sexuality.*
> *For the whole marvelous idea of male — femaleness.*
> *You made something beautiful, Lord,*
> *But I wonder, why did you make it so massive?*
> *My need to touch, to look, to fondle and merge,*
> *All the studies say we're constantly thinking of it.*
> *And sales of skin books show our great hunger.*
> *Why make sex so powerful, Lord?*
> *Like a 20 pound gland in a 100 pound body.*
> *Did you mis-engineer, Lord?*
> *Or are we mis-directed gluttons?*
> *Why must we keep grabbing at it?*
> *It's got to be powerful, sure! To keep the species going,*
> *But if you had toned it down a little Lord,*
> *I'm sure I still would have gotten around to my part.*
> *You call me to walk around with temptations,*
> *To control the forces instead of becoming enslaved by them,*
> *To eat but not become a glutton,*
> *To love but not become obsessed,*
> *To achieve, to love others more than myself.*
> *Paradox: Your world is full of it.*
> *Tension and conflict,*
> *Drive against drive,*
> *And sex is full of paradox — Get yours but don't use each other.*
> *Live with your drives but care more about her.*
> *What you demand of me, Lord, is a soldier's alertness in treading a mine field.*
> *It's only possible close to You, for only You know where the death traps are. And where the deepest love is."*

He's right. The solution is simple, but it's hard. It's easy, but tough. Lust is so strong that you can never overcome it on your own. You must lean heavy on the Lord and tap into His power in order to know victory. And when you begin to fill your mind with the mind of God, when you tap into the energy of His Spirit, you will find that lust and all of his allies will systematically be crowded out of your life.

So reconnect with God. Reject the rationalizations, remove from yourself any and every possible compromise. Then seek His face, draw upon His strength and rely on His power.

NOTES

[1] Magic Johnson, with Roy S. Johnson, "I'll Deal With It," *Sports Illustrated*, November 18, 1991, pp. 21-22.

[2] Ken Davis, *How To Live With Your Kids When You're Already Lost Your Mind*, p. 142.

[3] See Dick Polman's "Centerfold being shifted at Playboy," *Chicago Tribune*, Section D, Tuesday, May 7, 1985.

[4] Frederick Buechner, *Godric* — source unknown.

[5] Alfred Edersheim, *Bible History of the Old Testament* (Grand Rapids: Eerdmans, 1972 reprint), Vol. III, p. 174.

[6] John Taylor, in *Dictionary of Quotable Definitions*, Eugene E. Brussell, Ed. (Englewood Cliffs, NJ: Prentice-Hall, 1970), p. 347.

[7] Used by Permission of the Author.

CHAPTER SIX

When Your Faiths Don't Mate
EXODUS 4:21-26

A Roman Catholic girl was dating a Southern Baptist boy, and, after several dates, it was obvious that the two were getting quite serious. So the girl's mother sat her down and had a serious heart-to-heart talk.

Going straight to the point, she said, *"Honey, you realize, don't you, that Catholics don't marry Baptists? And that Baptists don't marry us Catholics? Honey, you're going to have to end this relationship."*

Her daughter cried, *"But momma, it's too late! I've already fallen in love with him! Can't we do something?"*

Seeing the pained look in her daughter's eyes, she thought for a moment, then said, *"Sure! We'll just talk this boy into taking catechism classes. That's it! We'll make a good Catholic boy out of him! Then you can get married!"*

It didn't take a lot of talking. This boy loved that girl so much, he would have done anything to please her. So he went through catechism, the wedding date was set, the announcements were mailed, and the church was reserved.

But then, about a week before the wedding, momma's little girl came in from an evening out with her betrothed, with huge, crocodile tears just spilling down her cheeks. She cried out, "Momma! It's all over. Call the priest. Cancel the wedding. Call the guests. I'm not getting married!"

The stunned mother said, "I don't understand. What's the matter? I thought we sold the boy on being a good Catholic!"

The daughter tearfully replied, "We did, momma! That's the problem! We sold him too good. He's decided to become a priest!"

According to Judy Petsonk and Jim Remsen, authors of *The InterMarriage Handbook*, marriages such as the one illustrated in that story are becoming quite commonplace. As barriers of religious prejudice and tradition tumble, as our American culture becomes more and more secular by nature, as religion is viewed as less and less determinant in people's lives — interfaith marriages have proliferated.

For example, the percentage of Jews "marrying out" (as they term it), has shot up from 6 percent thirty years ago to a current level of somewhere between 24 and 40 percent. The number of Jewish-Christian couples in the United States has topped five hundred thousand and is growing by about forty thousand a year.

"Today, half of all Catholics are choosing non-Catholic mates. That's up from 40 percent in 1981 and nearly double the percentage of 30 years ago." So reports sociologist Dean Hoge of Catholic University.[1]

Some call this social shift a severe source of family strife, while others consider it a model of religious tolerance. Still others view this trend as a threat to the orthodoxy of the faith. But the one thing that seems to be agreed upon by both proponents and opponents alike is that those who choose this course inevitably find themselves facing many pitfalls. For the truth is: Religious, cultural and philosophical differences do remain. And the pull of family tradition has not died.

And although the purveyors of political correctness love to talk about *"religious preference"* as though a religion was something you shopped for — like a new car or a brand new outfit

When Your Faiths Don't Mate

— although religion is often treated as though it were essentially a matter of taste or of style — ***the fact is, most people do not so much choose a religion as they are chosen by a religion.***

Some people are chosen by a religion by virtue of the culture into which they were born. Their ethnicity, their familial heritage is what determines their faith.

Others are chosen by a religion because the Spirit of God found them and pulled them right into fellowship. These are those who love to sing, *"I once was lost, but now am found."*

Do you see the potential for conflict here? On the one hand, if the *politically correct* crowd is right — and religion is merely a choice, a preferential decision based on a predetermined list of options — then an interfaith marriage might just work! Because all you have to do is sit down and negotiate with your spouse those items which offend and which might cause potential conflict and you just root them out!

I read of one mixed couple who made the following prenuptial deal: *"If you agree to have our children baptized, I'll agree to raise them Jewish."* Which makes sense, I suppose, if your religious convictions are somewhat akin to your opinions about exercise or diet. If joining a church for you is much like choosing a fitness club — if it's merely a matter of services rendered and the kind of atmosphere that is preferred — no problem!

However, if religion for you is *not* a preference — if you feel that in fact you have been chosen (and that this choosing has determined for you your eternal destiny) — the stakes are much, much higher. And if you believe that the Deliverer you worship is "the Way, the Truth and the Life" — and that "no one can come to the Father except through Him" — then you will endure enormous heartache believing that your spouse, and even your children, those in this world that you love the most, will never see the Kingdom of heaven.

I agree with David Neff:

"In our rush to accommodate the niceties of modern culture, we have failed to repair the hedges around

Christian marriage and to steer young adults away from unequal yoking. It is time not only to recall the rules of yesteryear, but to articulate clearly a theology of Christian marriage that places united service to the kingdom of God once again at its center."[2]

GOD'S COVENANTAL ARRANGEMENT WITH ISRAEL

Now that may not be a *politically* correct statement — but it is a *theologically* correct statement. For the position of God from the very beginning of His dealings with man was not that man made a choice to follow God, but that God made the decision to choose man. In fact, all the way back in Deuteronomy 7, just before the Israelites crossed over into the land God had promised them, Moses, that venerable old statesman, delivered one final message of caution. These, his beloved people, would be entering a land filled with pagans and unbelievers. And in Moses' warning, he begins with a reminder.

"The LORD did not set his affection on you and choose you because you were more numerous than other peoples" (Deut 7:7a).

Note that: He chose you; you didn't choose Him.

" . . . for you were the fewest of all peoples. But it was because the LORD loved you" (Deut 7:7b-8a).

That's why you have been the recipients of His favor!

"Know therefore that the LORD your God is God; he is the faithful God, keeping his covenant of love to a thousand generations of those who love him and keep his commands" (Deut 7:9).

**"Therefore, take care to follow the commands, decrees and laws I give you today. If you pay attention to these laws and are careful to follow them, then the LORD your God will keep his covenant of love with you, as he swore to your forefathers. He will love you and bless you and increase your numbers. He will bless the fruit of your womb, the crops of your land — your grain, new wine and oil — the calves of your herds and the lambs of your flocks in the land that he swore to your forefathers to give you. You will be blessed more than any other people . . ." (Deut 7:11-14a).

And he goes on and on, describing the multiplied blessings that God's people will know if only they follow His commands. Read it for yourself; it's absolutely fascinating. The command that is of interest to us is found a few pages later in Deuteronomy 11.

> "Love the LORD your God and keep his requirements, his decrees, his laws and his commands always" (Deut 11:1).

> "Observe therefore all the commands I am giving you today, so that you may have the strength to go in and take over the land that you are crossing the Jordan to possess, and so that you may live long in the land that the LORD swore to your forefathers to give to them and their descendants, a land flowing with milk and honey" (Deut 11:8-9).

> "So if you faithfully obey the commands I am giving you today —to love the LORD your God and to serve him with all your heart and with all your soul — then I will send rain on your land in its season, both autumn and spring rains, so that you may gather in your grain, new wine and oil. I will provide grass in the fields for your cattle, and you will eat and be satisfied. Be careful, or you will be enticed to turn away and worship other gods and bow down to them" (Deut 11:13-16).

If that happens, says the Lord . . .

> "Then the LORD's anger will burn against you, and he will shut the heavens so that it will not rain and the ground will yield no produce, and you will soon perish from the good land the LORD is giving you. Fix these words of mine in your hearts and minds; tie them as symbols on your hands and bind them on your foreheads. Teach them to your children, talking about them when you sit at home and when you walk along the road, when you lie down and when you get up. Write them on the doorframes of your houses and on your gates, so that your days and the days of your children may be many in the land that the LORD swore to give your forefathers, as many as the days that the heavens are above the earth" (Deut 11:17-21).

Now because we benefit from perfect 20/20 hindsight vision, we know that Israel failed to keep that command. And we also know that the enticement **"to turn away"** came when the sons of Israel began to marry foreign women, who, in turn, began to bring into Israel's camp their pagan idols and false gods. And thus began the downfall of God's chosen people.

God had made it abundantly clear that Israel was to remain exclusively devoted to Him. This nation was to maintain her rigorous spiritual distinctives. There was to be no blurring, no blending of their spiritual heritage. They were to be a separated, exclusive people. Not because of prejudice, not because the Jews were better than anyone else — but because God had chosen them and had commanded them to be separate unto Him and Him alone.

Joshua, when he took the reigns of leadership from Moses, reminded the people, **"If you forsake the LORD and serve foreign gods, he will turn and bring disaster on you . . ."** (Josh 24:20). And that's exactly what happened. And it still does. I frequently get letters and have conversations with those who are struggling because of an unequally yoked marriage. And those who write, those who call, are often sincere believers who chose to marry someone who has no commitment to Christ at all. And as a result, they face unimaginable hardship and compromise. I talked to a woman who said that life for her is like living under a *"huge, dark cloud."* She said that she faces *"incredible pain."*

Someone has said, *"If you're a child of God and you marry a child of the devil, you're certain to have trouble with your father in-law."* And he's right. Satan takes great pleasure in using any open door we provide him. And a spiritually-mixed marriage is one such open door.

Now despite God's very clear command, it's interesting to me that some of God's most notable heroes blew it in this very regard. And what I want you to see is that the pain God promised is exactly what they faced.

SOLOMON AND HIS MANY FOREIGN WIVES — An Unspiritual Bond Can Lead To Spiritual Compromise.

For example, the nation of Israel, for years, had known nothing but enormous success. That is, until **SOLOMON** began marrying foreign women. Here was a king who was wiser, richer, more powerful than any other monarch on earth! He was a man of incredible gifts and power! In all of human history, there has never been another kingdom quite like the kingdom of Israel, nor another king quite like Solomon.

But Solomon blew it. And when he did, he became an eternal reminder that *if you form an unspiritual bond, that bond can lead you into spiritual compromise.*

According to 1 Kings 3, Solomon **"made an alliance with Pharaoh king of Egypt and married his daughter."** Now that wasn't supposed to happen! It was an obvious breech of God's command. *Solomon, you're the wisest man on earth! You had a choice, at one time, to receive from God anything you wanted — and you chose wisdom! So why did you make such a foolish decision now? Why did you decide to do what is so obviously wrong?*

Well, Dad did it (I'll show you that in a minute)! *And he got away with it! Besides, what's the big deal? So she's a pagan! So she has a few idols. It'll all work out.*

NO IT WON'T. BECAUSE SHE'S NOT SAVED, SOLOMON. It's the beginning of the end, big guy. It's just the foothold Satan needs to bring you down.

And sure enough, by chapter 11, Solomon, now held captive by his own lust, has married 700 wives and 300 concubines in direct violation of God's command! One thousand women, most of them pagan! Even though Scripture clearly commanded that Israel's king **"Must not take many wives."** Why? **"Or his heart will be led astray"** (Deut 17:17). Well that's exactly what happened. Can you believe it? 1 Kings 11:6 says, **"Solomon did evil in the eyes of the LORD."** He even allowed those wives to **"burn incense and offer sacrifices to their gods"** (1 Kgs 11:8).

And sure enough, just as God had promised, as soon as Solomon died, Israel was torn asunder by civil war — and was eventually led into captivity.

The downfall continued under King Ahab, who foolishly married the evil Jezebel, daughter of the Senior Pastor of the First Church of Baal up in Sidon. And Jezebel, not content to worship her tin god in privacy — but hell-bent on making Baal worship the official religion of Israel — brought untold suffering to a nation already reeling under God's divine judgment. Not the least of which was three years of famine and drought. In direct fulfillment of God's warning, the heavens were shut because of this sin.

What's going on here? What are God's chosen people doing making alliances with and arranging marriages with and establishing partnerships with unbelievers? Especially when God so clearly said, *Don't do that!*

MOSES AND ZIPPORAH — A Spiritually Divided Home Can Lead To Spiritually Confused Children.

Then there's **Moses and Zipporah.** You remember Moses. Rescued from the Nile by Pharaoh's daughter, raised in Pharaoh's palace, educated in the finest schools in the land — Moses had been preparing his entire life to free Israel. The trouble is, at age 40, he got impatient and rushed God's plan. He murdered a man and was banished to the wilderness for 40 years. While in exile, Moses agreed to marry Zipporah. I don't know why he didn't trust God to bring him a mate from among his own people. He just didn't. And when she gave birth to a son, **"Moses named him Gershom, saying, 'I have become an alien in a foreign land'"** (Exod 2:22).

But then, having just encountered that amazing burning bush, Moses prepares to return to his homeland. He heads back to Egypt to do the job in the energy of the Lord that he had tried before to do in the energy of his flesh.

> **"Now the LORD had said to Moses in Midian, 'Go back to Egypt, for all the men who wanted to kill you are dead.' So Moses took his wife and sons, put them on a donkey and started back to Egypt"** (Exod 4:19-20a).

Now don't read too quickly. Something very strange happens in verse 24:

> **"At a lodging place on the way,** [The phrase **"lodging place"** doesn't mean Holiday Inn, it was more like a KOA campground.] **the LORD met [Moses] and was about to kill him"** (Exod 4:24).

Don't you find that strange? *God commands him to go to Egypt. He obeys God, and on his way, God plans to kill him*! Can you imagine? *Why would God do such a thing?*

Well, as we'll see in a moment, it's because Moses had failed to circumcise his youngest son. Circumcision was not just a physiological procedure; it was a uniquely Hebrew symbol of obedience. It was first practiced on Abraham and served as a covenant sign for all of his descendents. In fact, in Genesis 17, there is a sentence of excommunication pronounced on anyone who neglects doing the deed. And yet Moses, although he had circumcised his oldest son, had simply neglected to circumcise his youngest.

Perhaps it was because his non-Israelite wife was opposed to it. Or maybe his father-in-law thought it was cruel and unnecessary (although Midianites were also descended from Abraham)? And Moses, in his present condition — perhaps decided it wasn't worth the hassle. Despite the fact that God had commanded it — Moses opted for the path of least resistance. I mean, after all, it was no big deal! Besides, who would know?

God knew. And to God, it was not trivial, it was vital. So he punished Moses just as He had promised. Bringing Moses to the very precipice of death, He somehow communicated WHY He was displeased, which is why . . .

Behind the Tent Flaps

> "... Zipporah took a flint knife, cut off her son's foreskin and touched [Moses'] feet with it. 'Surely you are a bridegroom of blood to me,' she said. So the LORD let him alone. (At that time she said 'bridegroom of blood,' referring to circumcision.)'" (Exod 4:25-26).

I take it that she grudgingly performed the ritual in order to save her husband's life. But she still didn't like it one bit. In fact, she called him a bloody husband, took her two boys and stomped back home to live with daddy in Midian.

That's the way things can happen in a mixed marriage. What seems at first to be a simple, logical arrangement — when kids come along — can become an emotional mine field. Only then is the couple forced to face the reality that they avoided throughout their courtship, their wedding, and those early years when they were childless. They now realize the importance of giving their children a spiritual heritage. They want to give their kids the solid footing that they themselves had known. But with that desire come the inevitable questions:

> *Will the baby be baptized or dedicated?*
>
> *Will we celebrate Christmas or Hanukkah?*
>
> *Will he be circumcised?*
>
> *Will he attend religious school?*
>
> *If yes, what faith?*
>
> *And where will we go to church?*
>
> *And how will we make these choices?*

The sad truth is, **a spiritually-divided home can lead to spiritually-confused children.**

> "Although her Italian-Catholic father and Jewish mother left the decision up to her, Angela reports that she still feels paralyzed. *I tell you, I feel like a traitor. If I go to a synagogue, I'm betraying my father. If I go to church, I think how my mother would object. I feel like I can't go to either one!*"[3]

Betty says, *"I feel culturally and intellectually Jewish, but spiritually and religiously Catholic. It's a fine line that I walk.*"[24]

Victoria recalls, *"When my father learned that I'd decided to live as a Jew, he said, 'I'm delighted, but don't tell your mother I said that.'"*[25]

And what makes such confusion tragic is when one or both spouses are convinced that unless their faith is adopted, their children will not be saved. Scripture says, **"Happy is the man whose quiver is full of them."** But miserable are they who fear that their marital choice could lead to the damnation of their own children.

DAVID AND MICHAL — An Interfaith Marriage Can Result In Unwanted Interference From The In-Laws.

Talk about in-law problems! I mentioned earlier that **David** had also married an idol-worshiper. And her father so thoroughly despised David that he actually approved of the marriage just so he could use her to get to him. In fact, he even tried to kill David. Thankfully, **Michal** (David's wife) would have nothing to do with that plan. The trouble is, she used an idol to save him. Evidently, she too, was an idol-worshiper.

By the way, that's another pitfall in a mixed marriage. The in-laws. The parents of a mixed marriage often feel guilty and humiliated, even betrayed by the choice of their child. They accuse themselves of failing to raise him properly, and in a vain attempt to rectify their mistakes, they push for concessions: Where the wedding will take place and who will perform the ceremony. And when grandbabies come along, oftentimes the grandparents become far more intrusive than ever — simply because they don't want their grandbabies to be led astray like mommy and daddy were.

DAVID AND MICHAL — A Diversity In Religion Can Make It Difficult To Agree On A Particular Style Of Worship.

Now I happen to believe that it was daddy's displeasure that led Michal, ultimately, to criticize David's worship style. I say that because in the book of 2 Samuel, chapter 6, King David was leading the ark of the covenant triumphantly back into Jerusalem. Now understand, David was enjoying what was, essentially, the spoils of military victory.

> "As the ark of the LORD was entering the City of David, Michal daughter of Saul watched from a window. And when she saw King David leaping and dancing before the LORD, she despised him in her heart" (2 Sam 6:16).

I mean, after all, she had grown up in the sophistication of the palace. Her daddy had been king, too. And David wasn't acting very king-like.

> "When David returned home to bless his household, Michal daughter of Saul came out to meet him and said, 'How the king of Israel has distinguished himself today, disrobing in the sight of the slave girls of his servants as any vulgar fellow would!'" (2 Sam 6:20).

Now keep this moment in context. David is at the height of his glory. He is worshiping the Lord and giving Him praise for the great victory of Israel! And right in the middle of his party — she blasts him. *"Way to go, hotshot. You looked like a real jerk out there!"* Which didn't set well with David. He shot right back . . .

> "David said to Michal, 'It was before the LORD, who chose me rather than your father or anyone from his house when he appointed me ruler over the LORD's people Israel — I will celebrate before the LORD. I will become even more undignified than this, and I will be humiliated in my own eyes. But by these slave girls you spoke of, I will be held in honor'" (2 Sam 6:21-22).

In other words, *"If you don't like it, there are some other women out here who do!"*

You see, another of the heartaches of a mixed marriage is:

How do you resolve worship?

What church to attend?

What level of involvement is acceptable?

How much will he let me give?

Will she mind if I get involved in a small group?

These are questions that spiritually-matched partners never have to deal with.

MR. AND MRS. JOB — An Unspiritual Spouse Can Offer Unwise And Destructive Counsel.

One more example: **Job and Mrs. Job.** Remember Job's heartache? The loss of his job, his children, and his health in one single day? The tragedy was aggravated even more by the attitude of Job's wife. When he needed spiritual support the most — she wasn't there for him. All she could muster was, *"Curse God and die!"* (Job 2:9). Remember? Which is yet another pitfall of the mixed marriage. *An unspiritual spouse can offer unwise and destructive counsel.*

GOD'S LOVING COMMAND TO MODERN BELIEVERS

Please understand, our heavenly Father is not some ogre who peers through the portals of heaven and discovers what it is that gives us pleasure, only to scurry back to the throne and scrawl out Commandment # whatever saying, *"Thou Shalt Not Do That Either!"* No! Sin is not sin because God wants to deprive you of a good time. In fact, sin is not sin because it affects God even in the least. *Sin is sin because of what it can do to you.* And that's why God gave Israel this command. He was trying to protect them from the disgrace and heartache I just described. And even more, what I haven't described. *And that's also why, when He ushered in the new covenant* — He continued to hold to His previously adopted position.

"Do not be yoked together with unbelievers" (2 Cor 6:14a).

Now don't go too far with this. Based on this verse, some believers won't even play softball with a pagan. Or pump gas at a pagan's station. Or live next door to a pagan. Hey, that's how Waco got started! And Jonestown. And a thousand other cults we've never even heard about. But that's not Paul's point! The word **"yoked"** references a closely-held union. A partnership that extends for a long period of time. In fact, the thought of this verse goes all the way back to Deuteronomy 22:10 which says, **"Do not plow with an ox and a donkey yoked together."**

You hitch a donkey and an ox together — and you're asking for trouble! The two are incompatible. They will drag each other down. You just don't do that!

I find two major applications from this verse:

First, you are not to be bound together with an unbeliever in a contractual partnership. Don't get into long-term business relationships with nonbelievers — that's the point.

And secondly — if you are saved, don't marry someone who is lost. If you do, you are **"unequally yoked."**

Paul even asks five relevant questions to help you see the wisdom in this command:

"For what do righteousness and wickedness have in common? Or what fellowship can light have with darkness? What harmony is there between Christ and Belial? What does a believer have in common with an unbeliever? What agreement is there between the temple of God and idols?" (2 Cor 6:14b-16).

You see, some things are essentially distinct and fundamentally incompatible. The saved simply CANNOT have partnership, fellowship, harmony, or agreement with the LOST. You're only asking for trouble by entering into such an arrangement.

Which means, young person, if you have your eye on somebody — if that somebody, though very polite, wonderful, handsome and affirming, isn't saved, then he's not God's choice for your life. You don't have to pray about that; you don't have to seek godly counsel. If he is not in harmony, agreement, and partnership with you spiritually — cut off the relationship right now. It is not God's will that you marry him.

Now before you cut it off, try to lead him to Christ. Talk about a key witness opportunity. Several years ago, Vanessa and I had a dear friend who was madly in love with an unsaved man. And he was a good man. He was thoughtful, kind — he had a wonderful servant's heart. But he wasn't saved. He asked her to marry him. She said that wished she could, but unless he was a believer she could not. Well, Donny came to faith, and I had the privilege of marrying them. They have a beautiful family today, and all of them are walking with God!

So you see, it CAN happen. But it must happen BEFORE marriage, not after. You have no right to plan a marriage unless the one you're planning to marry knows the Lord. Otherwise, you bind yourself to a lifestyle with which you don't agree, to a philosophy with which you have no harmony.

Now since that passage is so painfully clear — why is it that so many disregard its wisdom so emphatically? Let me offer a few of the reasons I have heard.

Some believers become unequally yoked because they weren't that spiritually motivated when they made their life's choice. Although they were raised in a spiritual home — they fell in love at a time when faith was mom and dad's thing. So the issue of differing faith didn't even come up. It wasn't even discussed.

The Wyatt family has a Saturday morning tradition. Dad cooks breakfast, Mom sleeps in, and the kids just sort of crawl out and watch cartoons or play Sega. And as soon as I whip up some homemade sausage gravy and biscuits, I yell down the hallway — and here they come! One Saturday just recently, I yelled, and everyone came — Joshua in a pair of shorts, Andrea in her PJ's, Vanessa in a T-shirt and jeans — and Jessica in a brand new church outfit. I mean, she was absolutely decked out! But it was Saturday! Vanessa said, *"Jessie, why are you so decked out on Saturday? Why did you put your very best clothes on for a bum-around day like today?"* Jessie shrugged her shoulders and said, *"I dunno. It just felt right!"*

A lot of people make their lifelong selection of a mate in the same haphazard manner. And because spiritual things don't seem all that important — they aren't even discussed.

Others become involved in a mixed relationship because they are in a period of rebellion against whatever their parents or even the church has taught them. Whatever mom and dad are for — that's what I'm against! Whatever the church teaches — that's what I don't believe! Now in my experience, some of that rebellion is understandable. It's not excusable, but it is understandable, because some churches take 2 Corinthians 6 too far. That was true in my experience. When I was in high school, I was taught that it was an unequal yoke to date anyone who did not attend my particular church. It wasn't just whether a kid was a follower of Jesus, mind you, but whether that kid went to MY church. Not even other churches of the same label as mine were good enough. It was MY church! And I watched as good and godly kids became so frustrated by such legalistic lunacy that they jumped ship and abandoned the faith.

Listen, Scripture knows nothing of such malarkey. The labels which tag Christians today were thoroughly unknown by the writers of Scripture. In the days of Acts, a believer was simply one who had confessed Jesus Christ as Lord — and having received Christ's payment for his sins, he was one who lived in obedience and submission to Christ's Lordship. And that's still the definition of a believer. So don't make this passage some whipping post for your particular label. That's not what Paul had in mind at all. This doesn't mean that different nuances of faith and practice can't cause conflicts in a marriage, particularly questions of where to attend church. However, Paul's definition of an unequal yoke was "with unbelievers."

Others simply weren't believers until after they were married. Now they're married, and their yoke is unequal. And, in most cases, unbearable.

Still others forged ahead, thinking that they will eventually

convert their lover. Which reminds me of the time a nervous bride asked her minister for help in calming her nerves just before her wedding. The minister had a sure-fire formula. *"As you come through the door, keep your eyes down,"* he advised her. *"Don't look around at the people. Keep your gaze fixed upon the aisle down which you will walk. When you are about halfway down the aisle, raise your eyes just a bit until you can see the altar and keep your gaze fixed there until you are nearly to the front, and then lift your gaze just the slightest bit until you see him — the one who is your beloved."*

The wedding march began, the doors opened before her, and there stood the beautiful young bride looking remarkably composed. People did wonder, however, as she passed them, about her muttering determinately under her breath, *"Aisle, altar, him." Aisle, altar, him."* Many young brides marry with that very intention. *I'll alter him!* Unfortunately it rarely works.

And some of you know that . . . now. Now that it's too late. But if it's not too late for you, remember what I said before: You have no right to move toward marriage, if your future mate is not in harmony with you spiritually. It's putting the cart before the horse, and it spells absolute disaster.

Finally, **some marry an unequal yoke because they're afraid they'll be forever single.** Better a bad mate than no mate at all.

I've heard that very fear spoken many times. *If this guy isn't God's choice for my mate — then who is? After all, I'm at the ripe old age of 23 — I'm dying on the vine! He's got to be the right one!*

No — if it's right, you won't have to force it. If he's the right one for you, he'll be an equal yoke. Otherwise, you're just racing ahead of God's plan. You're grabbing for whatever you think you want — but, let me tell you, our world is chock full of people who will gladly tell you: *What you will get is not what you're hoping for.*

I read the story of Mrs. Sharpe of Los Angeles, who takes her poodle, Jonathan, for a walk every night. One night a mugger attacked her from behind, shoved her to the ground, grabbed the plastic bag she was carrying, and ran off with the spoils of his crime. She suffered a broken arm but remained good-humored, explaining to police that the bag was used to clean up after Jonathan, after he did his poodle duty. She said, *"I only regret that I did not have more to give him."* You grab for someone who is not a believer — that's what you get, my friend. A baggie full of doo-doo.

I close with two words of counsel that desperately need to be retrieved in the Body of Christ:

First, if you are not yet married — do not, under any situation, marry an unequal yoke!

Now I realize that asking a young person in love to consider whether she really ought to get married is like asking a woman in labor if she really wants to have a baby! But the stakes are so high — I must ask. When you commit your life and your heart to another — it's for keeps. And if you don't do it God's way — there will be trouble.

Please! Don't force the issue! I could give you a list the length of my arm of couples who rushed ahead of God's plan and got married anyway — and after years of regret, they'd love to trade places with you.

The Apostle Paul told us that remaining single is the best option. But if that's not your gift, then by all means, marry! Just marry someone who knows and loves the Lord. If you think it's bad being single, try living with someone who doesn't share your faith. You don't know problems till you've been there.

But what about if you're already married in an unequal yoke? What then? I spoke with someone struggling with that very issue. There are times, she confessed, that she finds herself watching some of the men in our church as we worship — wondering what it would be like to have a husband who loves Jesus. She worries for her children and where their example of a godly male will be found. She agonizes when it's time for the offering, wishing that her husband would acknowledge her need to give. She longs for Christian fellowship, but the little she's able to do is already more than he wants her to do.

What do you say to a person like that? I have three words of counsel:

First: **STAY PUT, DON'T SNEAK OUT**

Check out 1 Corinthians 7:12-16 sometime. Paul tells unequal partners, *"If you are married to an unbeliever — and if he's willing to stay with you — you must stay with him."* Period. No alternatives. The reason, Paul says, is that your spouse will be sanctified by your presence. That doesn't mean that he will be saved just because you stick it out — but it does mean that by hanging in there, you provide for him a live-in witness for the cause of Christ. Paul even suggests that such unbridled obedience will lead to the holy lifestyle of your children. So even though God didn't want you to be in this situation, now that you are there — stay put!

Second: **LIVE THE LIFE, DON'T NAG AND WHINE**

Peter writes: **"Wives, in the same way be submissive to your husbands so that, if any of them do not believe the word, they may be won over without words by the behavior of their wives, when they see the purity and reverence of your lives"** (1 Pet 3:1-2). Did you hear that? **"Without a word."** In other words, don't quote Bible verses all the time. And don't nudge him with your elbow when you do get him to come to church. Just live the life — if you want to win him over, just be like Christ.

And then finally: **PRAY!**

Pray for his heart to change. Pray for your patience as he moves toward faith. And as you pray, claim **Proverbs 21:1**. It's a wonderful verse written to queens whose kings do not believe. Take a read and then hit your knees: **"The king's heart is in the hand of the LORD; he directs it like a watercourse wherever he pleases."**

NOTES

[1] *U. S. News and World Report* — Horizons, "Behind Rise in Mixed Marriages."

[2] David Neff, *Christianity Today*, 2/17/89.

[3] Leslie Goodman-Malamuth and Robin Margolis, *Between Two Worlds* (Pocket Books, Simon and Schuster, 1992)

[4] Ibid.

[5] Ibid.

CHAPTER SEVEN

He Who Dies with the Most Toys — Still Dies

ACTS 5

I couldn't believe my eyes — and yet there it was, right in my grubby little hands. I found myself reading and re-reading and reading again what looked for all the world like a birth announcement. In fact, that's exactly what it was. Only it wasn't your typical birth announcement. The front of the card was lined with bunnies jumping for joy in a field of wildflowers. The inside read as follows:

> *We Would Like To Share Our Excitement*
> *On The Delivery Of Our Baby Benz SL320*
>
> Place of birth: Stuttgart, Germany
> Length: 447 cm.
> Weight: 1859 kg.
> Proud Parents: Frank and Sally
> *[not their real names]*
>
> *AND WE COULDN'T BE HAPPIER!*

Lining the bottom of the card was a row of hearts followed by dollar signs, followed by more hearts and more dollar signs — which continued the entire length of the card.

What made this so hard for me to swallow is that I know one of those parents. And Sally used to have a very different set of values. At one time in her life, she understood the enormous difference between things that really matter and things that don't. But somehow, through the passage of time, Sally's been bitten. ***Bitten by the monster of greed.*** So that for her, nothing could be more exciting, more fulfilling, more satisfying than to slip behind the wheel of a sleek, German road car — complete with all the accouterments of style and grace, all the appointments that shout money and even power.

I held that card, which had arrived at my office, for what seemed like hours — and found myself internally shaken. I felt emotionally devastated because the lustful spirit of materialism had claimed yet another victim — and the victim was my friend.

I drove home, still quite moved by what I had seen — and honestly — also feeling a bit smug because Sally's problem certainly wasn't *my* problem.

In fact, I was feeling quite fine about myself until I walked into the family room and noticed that *The Sharper Image Catalog* had just arrived. Not realizing how vulnerable I was, I picked the thing up and started flipping through the pages. And if you've never seen *Sharper Image,* let me tell you: there's a lot of neat stuff in there.

I was particularly impressed by a computerized stroke analyzer that clips right onto your golf club. I thought to myself: *"If anybody's golf stroke needs analyzed, it's mine. Besides, it's only $119.95. That thing could really help my game."*

I flipped a few more pages and there it was: An electronic blood pressure monitor. Now, I've got high blood pressure, and it's so time consuming to have to pump that little bladder one squeeze at a time. And here was a little gadget that could *"automatically inflate at a touch."* Besides, it's only $149.95. And it's for my health!

Then there was the electric razor you can take to the shower with you. Which has never been a fantasy of mine, but it was only $249.95. What a deal!

He Who Dies with the Most Toys — Still Dies

Can I be honest with you? In less than five minutes, I had lusted all over that magazine! High-road Harry had taken a fall, and Sally had a passenger in the back seat of her new car. Oh, I could still justify my desires. After all, my stuff was for my health, or a time saver, or help for my much-deserved hobby! Besides, my price tags were much smaller than Sally's price tag. But no matter, just like Sally, I was wallowing in the pit of my own greed.

Let me show you some of the other things that I found myself wanting:

"Totally redesigned: The World's best massage recliner. Four massaging rollers travel slowly from the base of your spine to your head, stretching and relaxing back, shoulder, and neck muscles. A second pair of pressure-sensitive rollers adds soothing oscillations [I don't even know what that means, but it sounds wonderful, doesn't it?] *Push a button and innovative hydraulic action adjusts smoothly to any position. Inside the headrest, dual audiophile-quality speakers deliver superb fidelity and separation. An upgraded auto-reverse cassette play envelopes you in music. Only $2,595."*

And how about this one?

A portable sauna that *"snaps together in minutes to create a personal steam chamber that can ease tension, relax tired muscles and open pores to deep cleanse and rejuvenate the skin. Plugs into simple wall outlet. Only $1,295."*

Or how about a Wurlitzer jukebox, designed to replicate the appearance of the '40s but with the digital sound of the '90s. *"Only $7,995. Plus shipping."*

For Christmas, there was *"a six-foot tall decorative angel, covered with 3300 miniature lights. Guaranteed to create a spectacular display on your front lawn, driveway or walk this holiday season. Just $3500. One three-prong grounded extension cord required (not included)."*

Then there's the wristwatch spy camera, perfect for taking truly 'candid' shots of your friends and family. Just $199.95.

And how about a nifty Art-Deco stereo? Bang and Olufsen's Beosystem looks more like a fine sculpture than a high-tech audio system, but the genius is its convenience. *"Merely move your hand toward Beosystem, and smoked glass doors glide silently apart as infra-red sensors react to your intent. Soft side lighting comes on, illuminating a brushed-aluminum console."* WOW! And how much will you pay for the privilege of playing that scene from Ali Baba? "Open sesame?" Just $2,595.

Tired of reaching for a cold towel after a hot shower? This towel warmer can be yours for just $129.95.

Or how about a 5'6" gumball machine? It holds 9000 gumballs — not included. Only $1,995.

One more: Are you tired of crushing your piggies every time you take a midnight trip to the bathroom? Then why not buy a pair of lighted doggie slippers? Slip them on and the light automatically illuminates your path. Only $39.95, plus shipping and handling.

Now I had a lot of fun putting this together, but I want you to know something: Everybody who saw that list — to the person — *everybody* said at least once, *"You know, I'd like to have that." "I could use one of those!"* How about it? Is there anything on that list that turns your crank? *"That sauna would make my home what it ought to be!" "And that recliner? That's just what I need to relax after a hard day down at the office!" "Honey, where's my VISA card?"*

OHH! Money and the things money can buy are so powerful!

THE PROBLEM WITH POSSESSIONS

I read sometime ago that the top two toys of today's high-powered executives are: flip phones, which weigh less than a pound, are capable of data or fax transmission and can fit easily in a shirt pocket. They start at $400 each. Then there is the Mont Blanc pen, which retails anywhere from $150 to $100,000 (a solid gold and diamond pen). The most popular version is the black, cigar-shaped Meistersteuck, which costs

$395.[1] Now compare that to the two to a package Bic pen set at Osco, on sale "this weekend only!" for $1.59.

It's incredible! And yet, we just peel it off and plunk it down — because we're bitten! We've got the disease, right down to our toenails!

I don't care who you are or how spiritual you may be — money and the things that money can buy can literally clean your clock. Some studies show that over half of all divorces take place because of money matters. Other studies reveal the #1 topic of dispute between couples is money and how it will be spent.

Money. We go to school to find out how to earn it, spend 40-65 hours a week actually making it, peruse magazines and wander shopping malls countless hours trying to figure out how to spend it. We're constantly fretting that we won't have enough of it, so we scheme and dream, hoping to find ways to get more of it. We argue about it, we gamble for it, we take our own lives because we don't have enough of it, or we embezzle our employer in an effort to acquire more than we deserve. *Money is deadly stuff!*

PRINCIPLES REGARDING THE PROBLEM

And that's why our Lord Jesus, knowing just how deadly money can be — pulled some of His key men aside for a little confab one day. The result is what we call *The Sermon on the Mount*. What it really was, was a message straight from Jesus' heart. And do you know what He told those guys? Two things:

First, He taught them that **EARTHLY POSSESSIONS AREN'T WHAT THEY'RE CRACKED UP TO BE.**

He said, *"Guys, I don't know who fed you this garbage, but earthly possessions are deadly."* Actually, His exact words were: **"Watch out! Be on your guard against all kinds of greed!"** *Why Jesus?* **"For a man's life does not consist in the abundance of his possessions"** (Luke 12:15). Have you figured that one out, yet? Or are you, like me, still trying to put it together? Still occupied with accumulating a tall pile of stuff? Jesus said, *"Despite what you may have heard, that 'stuff' will never take you where you want to go."* And then He mentions several reasons why He says that.

First, because possessions do not lead to contentment. Jesus said,

> "Do not store up for yourselves treasures on earth, where moth and rust destroy and where thieves break in and steal" (Matt 6:19).

You see, money lies to us. Money says, "He who dies with the most toys, wins!" When the truth is, "He who dies with the most toys — still dies."

I heard of an ad in a newspaper sometime ago. An ad of a huge, ruby ring sold at Tiffany's in Beverly Hills. Listen: *"Ruby, of exceptional size: 17 carats. Brilliance and clarity. From our collection of rare, imported gemstone rings. Only $297,000."* Whew! It took guts for that copy writer to put the word "only" in there, don't you think? And the maddening thing, Jesus says, is that the person who buys that ring will take it home, and put it on — and in a matter of just a very few months? It won't satisfy anymore. Any more than Sally's Mercedes will thrill her once her car gets dinged at the grocery store.

Jesus is right: Things will never satisfy! Because cars rust and get dings in them, and rings get stolen and are lost. And besides, once it's finally yours, what's the big deal?

Terry Hershey writes,

> *"We live in a world where more is never enough. Coping mechanisms and consequences are evident. We cannot be content, so we fantasize about those who do 'arrive' by reading about lifestyles of rich and famous people; we sacrifice the values of our 'ordinary life' of relationships, family and personal solitude to pursue the ecstasy that will let us 'be somebody.'"*[2]

But listen to the words of a man who could buy and sell Donald Trump a thousand times. King Solomon could have financed this country's entire health care package from petty cash. Yet here's his assessment:

"He who loves money will not be satisfied with money, nor he who loves abundance with its income" (Eccl 5:10, NASB).

In other words, if you are driven by money, you will never be satisfied with what you now have. No matter how large the pile may be.

I love the way George Carlin puts it:

"Never has society had as much stuff as we do. We fill our homes with stuff. But they keep inventing more and more stuff and then advertising comes along and says we gotta' have this stuff, too!"

It's crazy! But it's that drive for more that kept Emmit Smith sidelined for nearly a month during the 1993 NFL campaign. Already making into the tens of millions from both salary and endorsements — he was not content until he became the highest paid running back in the NFL!

It's what prematurely ended the 1994 baseball season. And halted the start-up of the hockey season.

It's that same drive that causes the pathetic gambler to stand at a slot machine and drop in one quarter after another. Finally the bell rings and the whistle screams and he "strikes it rich" as $400 worth of quarters fall into the bin below. But it's not enough. It's NEVER enough, is it? That's why he takes the entire pile and puts it right back into the machine — cause he's going to make an even bigger killing this time.

Tim Kimmel, in his book *Little House on the Freeway*, writes,

Every time I take a shower I remember the inability of things to satisfy. My old shower head had always managed to get me completely wet and adequately clean. But I kept seeing an ad on TV showing people standing under a 'special' shower head. It spread the water around and sent it flying in pulsating, rhythmic gyrations all over their backs. The people on the commercial were always smiling and laughing. I thought about my shower. It didn't make me

> *smile or laugh. It didn't relax my neck. It just managed to get me completely wet and adequately clean. I had to have one of those shower heads that made taking a bath a holiday. The new shower head cost me about 5 times more than the one I took off but my back is worth it, right? I bought this new necessity for happiness about 9 years ago now. The last time I turned the dial from normal to pulsating was about 8 years, 11 months and 3 weeks ago. Mainly it has served as a humble shower. But it does a great job of getting me completely wet and adequately clean.*[3]

Can you identify with that? How many times have we bought something, saying to ourselves, *"Man, when I get that, then I'll be happy."* But it never happens. Because possessions can never lead to contentment.

No, the truth is, possessions can mean an increase in problems. Paul told Timothy:

> **"People who want to get rich fall into temptation and a trap and into many foolish and harmful desires that plunge men into ruin and destruction. For the love of money is a root of all kinds of evil. Some people, eager for money, have wandered from the faith and pierced themselves with many griefs"** (1 Tim 6:9-10).

He's right. Consider just some of the fallout of a materialistic spirit:

For one, materialism literally explodes childlikeness, the very quality Jesus said is essential for kingdom citizenship. You see, rich people aren't worried about where their next meal will come from; they worry about what it will taste like and the ambience in which it will be enjoyed. Rich folk don't concern themselves with adequate shelter and clothing either; they're much more consumed by style and fashion — and adequate square footage. And they're not so much concerned with the worship of God as they are with the style of the service and the aesthetics of the architecture. You see, money shifts our attention from the elementary things of life, to another dimension. The wonder of simplicity is destroyed, and we wander from the simple faith which saved us.

Materialism also begets arrogance. Which is why Paul said to Timothy, **"Command those who are rich in this present world not to be arrogant"** (1 Tim 6:17a). Because that's the tendency! Prosperity breeds arrogance, insensitivity, self-satisfaction, and self-praise.

Which is why the Psalmist wrote:

> **"Do not lift your horns against heaven; do not speak with outstretched neck. No one from the east or the west or from the desert can exalt a man. But it is God who judges: He brings one down, he exalts another"** (Ps 75:5-7).

In other words: *If things are going your way right now, if everything you touch turns to gold, if you have more money than you know what to do with — don't toot your own horn. It's not because of you. God, for whatever reason, in infinite wisdom, has chosen to exalt you.* You are merely a grateful recipient of His abundant blessings.

Jesus warned the church at Laodicea:

> **"You say, 'I am rich; I have acquired wealth and do not need a thing.' But you do not realize that you are wretched, pitiful, poor, blind and naked"** (Rev 3:17).

The same could be said for many today. Please understand — we're the rich, OK? It's easy to think that this message applies to someone else. But I say to you, if you own a car — you're a member of the world's upper class. If you own a home you are more wealthy than 95% of all the people on this planet.

Materialism can also enslave its captives. You see, that's the problem with money. Money can buy tons of comfort, but not one ounce of contentment. Profits, dividends, investments, interest benefits, and capital gains only whet the appetite for more.

It's like the woman who had been instructed by her husband that there was no money for any additional purchases this month. In fact, as she was going out the door to meet her friends at the mall, her husband said, "Look, but don't buy." A few hours later, she came home with a new dress.

"What's this?" her husband fumed. "I thought I told you to look but not buy!"

"Well," she explained, "I saw this lovely dress and thought I'd try it on, and when I did the devil said, 'It sure looks good on you.'"

"Right then you should have told him, 'Get thee behind me Satan,'" her husband shouted.

"I did," she answered, "but when he got behind me he said, 'It sure looks good from the back, too.'"

You see, the more you feed on "the good life," the more you become owned by your possessions. Like a habit-forming drug, things start controlling your heart. And that responsive spirit you once had toward the things of God? It's gone! And just like the **Rich Young Ruler**, when God makes His appeal to your heart, you find yourself walking away in sadness — because you've got too much stuff to let any of it go!

And those so held are just as addicted to their stuff as a miserable crack addict writhing in some scummy alley is addicted to his stuff.

Case in point? Robert Jacoby, former president of Sunrise Savings and Loan (now insolvent) who stated, *"I have a pretty wife, a Jaguar, a Mercedes, a beautiful home, and a yacht. I want a Ferrari, a bigger house, and a bigger boat."* Now, with an attitude like that, how secure do you think his wife feels?

Speaking of insolvent savings and loans — Jesus also told His men that *possessions are as transient as the wind.* Remember His words?

"Do not store up for yourselves treasures on earth, where moth and rust destroy, and where thieves break in and steal" (Matt 6:19).

Follow the thought pattern. He said, *"If you put your wealth into clothing . . . "* Now that's exactly what many in that day did. They would sew golden threads into their garments. They would attach precious jewels in conspicuous places. *"If you do that,"* Jesus says, *"the moths will just eat it all up!"*

He Who Dies with the Most Toys — Still Dies

"And if you put your wealth into grain and other foods, rodents will just come along and rust it out." The word literally means *to eat*. It's a reference to insects or mice or rats getting into a barn and eating up a farmer's profits!

"And if you put your wealth in a bank, or in a shoe box under your bed — why, someone will just come along and steal it!" To give yourself to the piling up of earthly possessions is to live in perpetual insecurity. Let's face it: Even in our days of mothballs and insecticides and rat poison and mouse traps and rustproof paint and burglar alarms — we still face the loss of material things, don't we?

The fact is: Bread still molds, cars still rust, clothes still fade, homes still deteriorate, stock markets still crash, banks still fail, health still fades, jobs still evaporate, banks still close . . .

Solomon was right! **"Cast but a glance at riches, and they are gone, for they will surely sprout wings and fly off to the sky like an eagle"** (Prov 23:5).

Haggai agreed. He pointed to the futility of possessions, when he said, **"You earn wages, only to put them in a purse with holes in it"** (Hag 1:6b).

And if you don't believe that, just ask the people of Laguna Beach. Watching the devastation caused by the California wildfires of 1993, I called one of my friends who lives in Orange County, to see if he and his family were okay. Bruce told me that he spent the entire night standing on his front lawn, wondering when the flames would turn his direction. His home is filled with soot and ashes. It was spared, but just barely. *"It was an unbelievable night,"* he said. Hundreds of others weren't so lucky. Dozens of million dollar homes were instantly reduced to mere piles of ashes.

That's the way it is with riches. And even if you manage to escape this wildfire, even if you are able withstand the next pink slip assault at your place of employment, when you die — all the toys you have amassed won't make one lick of difference. I've never seen a hearse pulling a U-Haul. I've never seen a corpse driving a Mercedes or carrying a portable sauna. People, we come into this world empty-handed and we leave the same way!

Which brings me to the second of Jesus' two principles: Jesus said, **HEAVENLY POSSESSIONS ARE THE MORE EXCELLENT TREASURE.**

> **"Do not store up for yourselves treasures on earth, where moth and rust destroy, and where thieves break in and steal. But store up for yourselves treasures in heaven, where moth and rust do not destroy, and where thieves do not break in and steal"** (Matt 6:19-20).

Now **"treasures on earth"** describes anything that carries a price tag. Any of the stuff that man has created, invented, packaged — any of the type of equipment we've talked about today — that's earthly treasure. It's the kind of stuff you have to buy insurance for. You have to lock it up and protect it with intricate alarms. These things are the **"treasures of earth."** And Jesus says, *"Don't go after that stuff!"*

Please understand, Jesus is not saying that having things is wrong. Because it's not! Neither is He saying, *"If you have money you shouldn't enjoy it!"* Paul told Timothy, **"Command those who are rich . . . to put their hope in God, who richly provides us with *everything for our enjoyment!*"** (1 Tim 6:17).

What He IS saying is: *"Stop selfishly piling up huge mounds of possessions just for you!"* That's what He's assaulting. Not having stuff, but lavishly accumulating more and more stuff — just because "I want to have it!" It's the insensitive hoarding of things *for me* — that's the problem! When it's just for me, for *my* pleasure, for *my* fulfillment — that's greed. And Jesus said:

> **"Where your treasure is, there your heart will be also"** (Matt 6:21).

So how about it? *Where is your heart? Where is your treasure?* Listen, If you want to go after treasures — go for it! But go for the stuff that lasts! No, there's nothing inherently wrong with earthly wealth, but if you're going to go after something — why not go after something that REALLY matters? Why not invest your STUFF in *ETERNAL* TREASURE?

He Who Dies with the Most Toys — Still Dies

If you're going to give yourself to something — why not make it something that can never be touched! NEVER! You see, that's the beauty of God's deal. When you **"store up treasures in heaven,"** you have God's absolute guarantee of security. Because in heaven, moths aren't allowed. The pearly gates are rustproofed. And thieves are no match for Peter's 24-hour, seven day a week security system.

So doesn't it make sense to put your treasure where it can never be lost, never be stolen, and never, ever lose its shine? Jesus said, *"If you'll do that . . . if you'll 'seek first' my kingdom and my righteousness, if you'll invest in eternal treasures and not just the moth-eaten variety — all these* [other] ***things will be given to you as well"*** (Matt 6:33).

In other words, if you determine in your heart to give — if you make the pleasure of the King and the advancement of His kingdom paramount in your heart and focus — you will receive from Him an iron-clad guarantee of His divine security. Everything else you will need in this life and in the life to come — *will be yours!*

And even more than that, the very fact that you are giving some of it away will help keep your heart on target. Giving helps you remember the words of Jesus:

> **"Watch out! Be on your guard against all kinds of greed; for a man's life does not consist in the abundance of his possessions"** (Luke 12:15).

You can have it all, my friend, but not have what matters. You can possess everything you have ever wanted, but you still won't have what makes life work!

Several years ago a statement was made that has never left me. The man who was speaking said,

> *"It is better to fail in a cause that will ultimately succeed than to succeed in a cause that will ultimately fail."*

There are a lot of people in our culture who are in a mad pursuit for what is, ultimately, a failed project. It is to these people I offer the words of the late Malcolm Forbes, who said,

Behind the Tent Flaps

"If there is a next life, people like me had better hope the devil is not as bad as he's been painted." Well he is, Mr. Forbes. But then again, I guess I don't have to tell you that. You know the truth now. You spent your entire life serving money, and now you're spending eternity regretting such a foolish choice.

Some ministers are uncomfortable talking about this subject. They harass and stress themselves out over a topic that is, arguably, one of the most touchy subjects that preachers are called to handle. But I never have been terribly uneasy taking this thing on. And I think it's because I am so thoroughly convinced that if God could get just hold of your wallet — He would probably have a pretty good hold on your heart, too.

So I urge you to do with your money what doesn't come naturally: I urge you to deny the natural human response to attain and keep and hoard, and instead, to chart a much more significant path — marked by giving and serving and sharing. Friend, your life is so much more than just what you have. And your eternal life will be of far more infinite value than anything you may possess here.

I agree with Coach Tom Landry, certainly one of the finest football coaches in NFL history. He said of the Cowboy team he used to coach:

> *"I have a job to do that is not very complicated, but it is often difficult: To get a group of men to do what they don't want to do so they can achieve the one thing they have wanted all their lives."*

That's what this chapter is all about. I am urging you to do what you don't really want to do — so that you can accomplish the only thing that really matters.

Are you interested in building eternal castles? Do you want to build up a pile of possessions that will stand the test of eternity itself? Then give. Giving back to the Lord is right and it is good. And if you want to get a handle on greed — if you want to keep your heart on target — one way to do that is to cheerfully acknowledge that none of this stuff is yours anyway. So you freely return it to the One to Whom it *does* belong.

But having said that, let me also say this — *GIVING IS NO GUARANTEE AGAINST GREED*. Just because you return to the Lord a chunk of your possessions doesn't mean that you, by virtue of that gift, have a handle on materialistic lust. Chances are good, you do not. Now don't take my word on that. Listen to the warning of Jesus. In Matthew 6, in the very same Sermon in which Jesus applauded the virtue of **"laying up treasure in heaven,"** He also said, essentially, *"But watch your motives. Or else even your giving can provide an opportunity for greed."* Look at how He puts it:

> **"Be careful not to do your 'acts of righteousness' before men, to be seen by them. If you do, you will have no reward from your Father in heaven."** (Matt 6:1).

This is a universal principle of Christian worship. When you do what you do unto the Lord — whatever that thing done might be — don't do it in some attempt to gain recognition. Don't play to the crowd. Don't seek man's applause. Don't parade your piety. That's the thought. *And how is it that men tend to do that?* One way is in our giving.

> **"So when you give to the needy, do not announce it with trumpets, as the hypocrites do in the synagogues and on the streets, to be honored by men. I tell you the truth, they have received their reward in full"** (Matt 6:2).

Now I can find no evidence that an actual trumpet was ever used in the temple. What I *have* discovered is that the offering boxes that were used were horn-shaped in design. That is, they were smaller at the top than at the bottom in order to discourage thievery. And according to *The Babylonian Talmud*, these offering boxes were called **"trumpets."** And what happened was — when the Pharisees gave, they would take their money, and instead of dropping in a dollar bill, they would take 100 pennies and slam dunk them right down the throat of those metal receptacles, and the coins would make such a racket that Jesus called it **"the sounding of the trumpet."**

Why did the Pharisees do that?

Do you really need to ask that question? So that everyone in the temple grounds would turn and go, "Wow!" That's why. So all the other worshipers would say, *"Goodness! Did you hear that racket? Brother Joseph is really diggin' deep today!*

Jesus said, *"When you give, don't do that."* Why? Because when you give, hoping to impress others with your giving — you are pandering to your greed. Just as much as if you dialed a toll-free number and ordered that portable sauna from *The Sharper Image.* Oh, it's a different kind of greed. A greed for recognition. Applause. The approval of men. But it's greed, nonetheless.

And Jesus said, *"When you do that, when you give and men praise you for your obvious generosity — their applause is your only reward."* The term, **"reward in full,"** is an accounting term. And it means "paid in full." Nothing more is owed. Jesus says, *"When you sound the trumpets, you'll get a reward alright. But not the reward you're looking for. Your reward won't come from God, but in the moment when those who see you begin their applause — that's it. So enjoy it while it lasts, cause that's all you're going to get!"*

Now the moral of the story is: When you give, don't dangle your check in the air before you drop it in the plate, don't scrawl out the numbers on your commitment card large enough to be read from the next county; and don't give expecting a plaque on the wall or a thank you in the church newsletter. Just give! Otherwise, greed is still your master. He adds:

"But when you give to the needy, do not let your left hand know what your right hand is doing" (Matt 6:3).

In other words, don't turn your giving plan into a long, drawn-out affair. Just make your decision and then move on. *Otherwise, your giving can result in pride* — a pride that makes you feel a bit too good about what you've just done.

Or it can result in greed. When you give too much concern to what you give — oftentimes, you can fall prey to prosperity theology. That's when you give, thereby obligating God to bring you a financial windfall! You put the money in the plate, fully believing that God will, because you have given, just load you up with His blessings.

Now it's true that God promises to bless those who give. But when your right hand knows too much about what your left hand is up to — *GREED REPLACES GENEROSITY.* And the whole purpose for giving is destroyed.

Others give, hoping to earn a good report on Judgment Day. They think that God will be so impressed by their charitable contributions, He'll just *have* to let them into the kingdom.

Still others give, hoping that their generosity will be noticed by the church leadership, and they will be given a place of special honor.

The trouble is, do you know what happens when your left hand and your right hand get together? SURE! Clap, clap, clap! And in that moment of self-applause and self-praise — *greed has gotcha!* So don't give "giving" so much air-time that you impress yourself or try to impress others. *That's greed in sheep's clothing.* And you will receive no reward from the Father. In fact, you will be harshly judged for your actions.

A PARABLE WHICH ILLUSTRATES THE PROBLEM

Case in point? How about Ananias and Sapphira? Let's travel to Acts 5 as we once again pull back the tent flaps and discover yet another biblical marriage that struggled — this time, in this whole arena of finances.

Actually, let's begin in chapter 4. During these, the early days of the church, many foreigners had come to faith in Christ while they were visiting Jerusalem. And because of their new-found faith, many, rather than returning to their homeland, decided to stay in Jerusalem so they could be near their brand new brothers and sisters in Christ. The trouble is, they couldn't support themselves.

And so, in Acts 4, we're told that many of the local believers had begun to voluntarily sell off portions of their possessions

Behind the Tent Flaps

and bring the money to the elders so that it could be distributed to whoever had need.

> **"There were no needy persons among them. For from time to time those who owned lands or houses sold them, brought the money from the sales and put it at the apostles' feet, and it was distributed to anyone as he had need"** (Acts 4:34-35).

It's a beautiful depiction of the generosity and selflessness which marked the early church.

> **"Joseph, a Levite from Cyprus, whom the apostles called Barnabas (which means Son of Encouragement), sold a field he owned and brought the money and put it at the apostles' feet"** (Acts 4:36-37).

According to Jesus, that beautiful act of generosity should have gone unnoticed. But it didn't. Somehow word began to spread. I don't know, maybe the church treasurer told somebody who told somebody — and it got out that good old Barnabas had done it again. I mean, he was always helping people, that's how he got his nickname. And now here he is, getting credit for something that should have never been known. What was supposed to be a private act of compassion — had become an opportunity for public applause.

As a result, by the time we come to Acts 5, **GREED HAS REARED ITS UGLY HEAD.** And an otherwise unknown couple, who evidently wanted to be elevated to a place of prominence in the church, a couple who apparently had entertained a problem with pride or who had some need for public affirmation — decided that they'd sell some land, too.

> **"Now a man named Ananias, together with his wife Sapphira, also sold a piece of property"** (Acts 5:1).

Now please understand — they didn't *have* to sell that land, they *wanted* to sell it. And just so it's clear — there was nothing wrong with their owning the land in the first place. *So what was so wrong about all this?*

Ananias and Sapphira kept back some of the proceeds, but they told Peter that they were giving everything they had.

Again, understand: They had every right to keep whatever portion they wanted. That's not the problem. In fact, they didn't have to give anything at all! They CHOSE to give! The trouble is, they wanted to receive the kind of notoriety Barnabas had received — but they also wanted their money. *So they lied.* They stood before Peter and told him that the money they gave was the entire amount they had received. To which Peter replied, **"you have lied to the Holy Spirit"** (Acts 5:3b). And again, **"You have not lied to men but to God"** (Acts 5:4b).

Do you see the problem? Ananias and Sapphira tried to position themselves as authentic, generous, selfless people. Just like Barnabas, they had given their all! *Oh no they didn't.*

"With his wife's full knowledge he kept back part of the money for himself, but brought the rest and put it at the apostles' feet" (Acts 5:2).

Note that: Sapphira was privy to the plan. And rightfully so. After all, she was part-owner in the land. My point is, not only did Ananias' left hand know what his right hand was doing — his mate also knew what he was doing. And with her full and complete approval, Ananias stood before Peter and dumped that money right down the throat of the TRUMPET! *"Yep! That's the full amount, Peter. We're giving it all, BABE!"*

Now here's where it gets painful . . .

"Then Peter said, 'Ananias, how is it that Satan has so filled your heart that you have lied to the Holy Spirit and have kept for yourself some of the money you received for the land? Didn't it belong to you before it was sold?'" (Acts 5:3-4a).

Gulp. *"Yes."*

"'And after it was sold, wasn't the money at your disposal?'"

Gulp. *"Yes."*

"'What made you think of doing such a thing? You have not lied to men but to God.'
When Ananias heard this, he fell down and died. And great fear seized all who heard what had happened.

Behind the Tent Flaps

Then the young men came forward, wrapped up his body, and carried him out and buried him.
About three hours later his wife came in, not knowing what had happened (Acts 5:5-7).

Evidently, when Ananias didn't come home for supper, Sapphira started getting worried. And as she looked for him, she decided to see if he was down at the church. Isn't that amazing? The judgment was so swift and so severe that her husband was dead and buried — and she didn't know a thing about it!

"Peter asked her, 'Tell me, is this the price you and Ananias got for the land?' 'Yes,' she said, 'that is the price.' Peter said to her, 'How could you agree to test the Spirit of the Lord? Look! The feet of the men who buried your husband are at the door, and they will carry you out also.' At that moment she fell down at his feet and died. Then the young men came in and, finding her dead, carried her out and buried her beside her husband" (Acts 5:8-10).

Who can read those words without concluding, as I'm convinced we should, that greed is deadly?

"Great fear seized the whole church and all who heard about these events" (Acts 5:11).

And it still does. To this day, we still struggle with the severity of God's judgment. Let's face it — *most of us have done far worse than these two did.* And yet they're dead while we're still living. *So why was it that God reacted so severely?* I think it's because God wanted to leave us an example. I think He intended to make a statement early-on concerning the awful stench of hypocrisy and greed. I think He wanted to tell the church right at the outset — and in no uncertain terms — that when we start pretending to be something we are not — we are treading in dangerous waters. He wanted us to understand that giving is nothing with which to trifle.

I say that because as soon as these two pretended to give it all — they were struck down! In that moment, when they tried to cover their greed, the truth of their lives was laid bare and they were killed. Why didn't they just say, *"Look Peter, we sold our*

He Who Dies with the Most Toys — Still Dies

land for $2,000, and we want to give $1500 to the benevolent fund — but we need to save back the other $500 so we can pay off Visa."

If they had, I'm absolutely convinced Peter would've said, "*No problem! It's your money! We just thank you for caring enough to give what you have given. God bless you.*" But because they wanted the same press coverage Barnabas got, they pretended to be better than they were. And they were struck down.

One evening, I was talking with some friends during *Nut Night*, an annual Halloween alternative event we have at our church. One of the guys was remarking about how hard this particular truth had been for him to apply. And how much he's been struggling with all the implications of greed and materialism in his own life. And as I listened, I became convicted by my silence. I realized that if I kept my mouth shut one minute longer — if I held back what I knew but what no one else in this conversation knew — this vulnerable, honest man would have assumed something very wrong about me. He would have assumed that I was better than I really am. That I didn't struggle like he struggles. And I couldn't let that happen. So slowly but surely, I pulled back the collar of my jacket and showed him the label — the brand name — of the jacket I was wearing. I thought he was going to have a coronary. You know what he found out about me? He found out that his big mouth preacher was wearing a jacket made by — boy, do I hate to admit this — *The Sharper Image*.

I didn't want to show him that. Anymore than I wanted to tell you that I did. I would much prefer to have him (and you) think I've got it all wired. *And that's what you prefer, too.* And that's why the average prayer time in your Bible study group sounds more like the census report for St. Mary's Hospital than an honest request for spiritual support.

Think about it: When was the last time you told your group that money is eating your lunch? When's the last time you admitted some wrong or impure motive? When's the last time someone thanked you for praying for them — and you sat there, knowing in your heart that you hadn't — but you nodded your head anyway? Why didn't you just say, *"I'm sorry, but I forgot to pray. And I don't want you to think I did, 'cause I didn't."*

Isn't it amazing how, when we're with other believers, we immediately slip on this mask of adequacy — when the truth is, we're not adequate? We've got some tough things happening in our home, but we don't want to tell anybody about it. We can't deal with our children, but we're not about to admit it. So someone says in the church foyer, *"How's it going?"* And we say, *"Wonderful!"* when it's not wonderful at all.

The story of Ananias and Sapphira is not only an historical event to be remembered, it is a relevant parable exposing our own continuing conflict with transparent honesty. Especially when it comes to money and the things that money can buy. Because everyone of us wants everybody else to think that we've got it under control.

One man has said, *"We'd all like a reputation for generosity, and we'd all like to buy it cheap."*⁴

As believers, we know that it's wrong to love money, but it sure keeps us warm at night. We're like **Joe Louis**, the late heavyweight champ, who said, *"I don't like money actually, but it quiets my nerves."*

There are other times when we experience outlandish urges toward downright extravagant generosity — and it feels so good to want to give so much — but then something about the wooing nature of cash always pulls us back.

We see things in the mall or in some magazine or in a new car showroom that we really, really want. But we don't get that model or that style. Not so much because we have a handle on materialism — no, that model is really what we want — but because we're afraid that someone might consider our choice garish, extravagant, or beyond the pale of Christian sensibility, we choose the lesser model. Just like Ananias and Sapphira, we play to the crowd. Or we strain to hear our own applause.

Some of us give, but not nearly to the level that we should. We just can't bring ourselves to give in such a sacrificial manner that might require an adjustment in our lifestyle.

We want to be together, but we're not. We want to impress ourselves and others with the fact that we have it wired, but we don't. We want to have and yet we want to give, too. *Oh, what a battle!*

POINTERS FOR PERSONAL VICTORY

May I share with you three truths that can help you rise above that battle? Here's the first: If you want to win the battle of greed, you must, with all diligence and vigor, **GUARD YOUR HEART.**

All the way back in 1893, Richard D. Armour was worth $50 million. Now that's not chicken feed in our day — but in his day? That was serious money! Armour had built a huge meat packing business from the ground up. He employed over 15,000 workers. And yet, despite his enormous success, Armour still went to work at 5:00 every morning and worked feverishly until 6:00 in the evening, at which time he came home, ate dinner, and went to bed. *"I have no other interest in my life but my business,"* he told an interviewer. *"I don't love the money. What I do love is the getting of money."*²⁵

Wrong! He loved the money. You see, Jesus said, *"Where your treasure is, that's where your heart is, too!"* In other words, we serve what we love. I wonder, *what do you serve?* Do you slavishly give yourself to the unbridled pursuit of money?

Tom Eisenman, in his book, ***Temptations Men Face,*** makes a powerful observation:

> *Money may be our most difficult obsession. No concept nor commodity is more deeply rooted in and driven by our emotional needs. Nothing in the world today is more available, acceptable, and heavily promoted.*
>
> *We may struggle with overeating; food is plentiful in America and available in exquisite variety, but we have*

some help from society to beat our gluttony. There is media pressure against overeating. We know about the health problems that result. We know that being fat is not a generally acceptable look today."

Alcohol abuse is similar. Alcohol is widely available in numerous forms. Like food, it is attractively advertised. There is also immense pressure from society to manage drinking. Everyone knows the health hazards associated with alcohol. Everyone knows the potential harm of drinking and driving, both to the drunk driver and to those he may injure or kill.

But there is no media campaign to help us control our consumptive materialism and manage our lust for money.[6]

And men, especially among those who have earned a good living and have the possibility of earning a better living, there is the constant subtle, slick, money temptation to get in over your head: more time and effort at the office. Longer hours — and if you work more than the next guy, your efforts could result in an even greater contribution to your family and future.

Jesus said, however, **"a man's life does not consist in the abundance of his possessions"** (Luke 12:15).

Listen to these relevant words of counsel:

"Do not wear yourself out to get rich" (Prov 23:4).

"Whoever loves money never has money enough" (Eccl 5:10).

"People who want to get rich fall into temptation and a trap and into many foolish and harmful desires that plunge men into ruin and destruction" (1 Tim 6:9).

"Keep your lives free from the love of money and be content with what you have" (Heb 13:5).

Charles Spurgeon framed the conflict this way: *"It is a very serious thing to grow rich. Of all the temptations to which God's children are exposed, it is the worst, because it is the one they do not dread. Therefore, it is the more subtle temptation."* Subtle because we don't think it can hurt us, when the truth is — it can destroy us! Just like **Ananias and Sapphira**.

So guard your heart, my friend. Guard your heart. *How do*

you do that? Well, a great place to begin is to ask yourself some very painful questions. Like these, for example:

Is my heart focused on things? Do I think about anything more than I think about things? How to pull off that latest deal, how to arrange the purchase of that new toy . . . you know the schtick.

Do I, at times, overload myself with worldly pursuits — having so many irons in the fire — that I barely find time for God?

Do I go without sleep trying to figure a way to close escrow, yet go weeks without any time alone with my Creator?

Would I be willing to part with my spiritual health, if it meant hitting it big in the marketplace?

Does my pulse quicken when I think about getting a bigger home?

Do I fly into a rage when I discover a ding in my new van?

Am I immediately offended and irritated when someone suggests I need to give some of my money away?

Am I regularly, systematically giving a big chunk of my income to the kingdom?

Jesus said, **"Where your treasure is, there will your heart be also."** Is your heart on earthly treasure? How you answer those questions can give you a painfully accurate read on where your heart is.

Here's a second word of counsel: **READJUST YOUR FOCUS.**

Jesus said, **"Seek first [my] kingdom and [my] righteousness, and all these things will be given to you as well"** (Matt 6:33).

In other words, get the proper perspective on all of this. Readjust your focus. I love what Coach John McKay said to his team years ago when he was still coaching USC. His team had just been demolished 51-0 by Notre Dame. McKay came into the locker room and saw a group of beaten, worn-out, thoroughly depressed football players who were not accustomed to losing. He stood on one of the benches and said, *"Men, let's keep this in perspective. There are 800 million Chinese who don't even know this game was played."*

We need a new perspective, people. We need reminded, for example, that the average American leaves about $150 a year in car seats, under furniture, and in pants pockets. Money that we just carelessly lose! Now couple that with the fact that the average person in the world only makes $135 a year. And you soon realize, we need a new perspective!

We also need reminded that in our frantic attempt to give our children what we didn't have — we're robbing them of what we did have.

Not that long ago, the Schwan man, a door-to-door food salesman, came by our home. It was school report card day, and as he and Vanessa were talking, he mentioned two of the most exclusive neighborhoods in the city where I live and said that they are both the absolute worst places on his route for kids being left home alone after school. He said he could ring doorbells as late as 7:00 and the kids would come to the door, their parents still not home, and they would say to him — *"Just a minute,"* and they'd bring back their report card for him to look at. He would look it over and tell them, *"Your parents must be really proud of you."* Their typical response? *"Oh, mom and dad don't have time to look at it. They just sign it and put it back in the envelope."* One child said, *"They don't care."*

Isn't that terrible? All because we're too busy out in the concrete jungle working to give our kids what we didn't have! And in the process, we're failing to give them what they need most — not a new Sega, not their own bedroom, not a full-ride to Harvard — but a mom and dad who will spend time with them. A mom and dad who understand what really matters.

Do you know I think? I think the worst thing you could do, parent, is leave a huge wad of money to your children! They need to earn their own money. They need to learn for themselves how to scrape and save and make a way for them and their families. And you rob them of that joy when you do it for them. You need to spend that money of yours. Or better yet, you need to give it away — investing lavishly in kingdom projects.

I heard the story of the rich Texan who was talking on the phone to his banker in New York. After several minutes of conversation, the Texan took a liking to the New Yorker, and said, *"I've got a great idea. Why don't I send my jet up to New York this weekend to pick up you and your wife? We'd like to have you join us at our son's ranch outside of Austin. He's got 100,000 acres of land stocked with quarter horses, purebred cattle, and exotic game. Yep, I'm real proud of my boy. He earned it all by himself."*

"It sounds like your son has been a very successful young man," replied the banker. "Just out of curiosity, how old is your son?"

"He's eight," replied the Texan.

"Eight!" said the shocked banker. "How on earth did an eight-year-old boy earn enough money to buy a ranch like that?"

The Texan replied, *"He got four A's and one B."*

We need a new perspective, people. We need to readjust our focus. We need to establish more spiritual goals for our kids and less material ones. We need to spend time teaching them and modeling before them the primacy of things spiritual, rather than constantly barraging them with things material.

I was thrilled sometime ago, when Dr. Marlon Jordan, a very busy dad — a man who has much better things to do with his time than drive halfway across town just to show me his nine-year-old son's school paper — did just that. The paper was entitled, *"Favorites."* It was a fill-in-the-blank paper, with an item listed on the left side of the sheet, then a blank space on the right for Eric to scratch out his answer. At first, his answers were quite typical. For example,

Behind the Tent Flaps

COLOR _____blue_____
PET _____dog_____
ICE CREAM FLAVOR _____grape sorbet_____
SPORT _____soccer_____
DAY OF THE WEEK _____Sunday_____
HOLIDAY _____Easter_____
THING TO WEAR _____Bulls shirt_____

But when my eyes saw the next line, I knew why Dad had come to see me. And I felt a lump beginning to develop in my throat.

THINGS I OWN _____Jesus Christ_____

There's a kid who has a head start on what life is all about. A kid who's lucky to have a mom and dad who care enough to teach him well. And if Eric continues guarding his heart — that "favorite" possession of his will provide him with riches that will never fade, spoil or rust.

In addition to guarding our hearts, if we're going to win this battle, we're also going to have to **DETERMINE OUR LOYALTIES.**

Jesus said, **"You cannot serve both God and Money"** (Matt 6:24b).

Someone has said that money is the substance that can buy us everything but happiness and take us everywhere but heaven. And isn't that true?

Heaven cannot be bought. Citizenship in the kingdom is not for sale! In fact, there are a LOT of things that money can't buy. Money can buy a hospital, but it can't buy health. Money can buy a house, but it can't make that house a home. Money can buy sex, but it can't buy love. Money can buy pleasure, but it can't buy happiness. Money can buy a bed, but it can't help you sleep. Money can buy tons of comfort, but not an ounce of contentment. Money can buy a crucifix, but it can't buy you a Savior.

No, there is only one Gate that can provide for your eternal salvation — and that Gate is not a turnstile. It's Jesus. Bob Dylan says that *You gotta' serve somebody.* Jesus said, **"You can't serve both of us."** So who will it be? Will you build castles that will surely crumble — or will you invest in a mansion that will shine for eternity?

Jim Judge made his choice. Judge is a successful surgeon who moved to Nairobi, Kenya to work in a medical clinic. In commenting on that decision, he said, *"I became acutely aware that I was more concerned with keeping leaves out of my swimming pool than I was with making a difference with my life. So I packed up my family and we moved to a country to minister to AIDS patients who were getting no treatment at all."*

Wow. Would you do that? If you were convinced that God was calling, could you sell it all — everything — and move to a foreign field of service? Or could it be that the things you have are already taking an edge off your commitment to the Father?

Jesus said, **"Watch out! Be on your guard against all kinds of greed; a man's life does not consist in the abundance of his possessions"** (Luke 12:15).

You may have everything you've every really wanted, but if you don't have Jesus, you don't have a thing that really matters.

If you do have Jesus? Please watch out! Don't let things turn your heart, blur your focus, or challenge your loyalty. Affirm before God and before your brothers and sisters in Christ that your relationship to Jesus, your relationship with your family, your health, your peace of mind — THESE ARE SO MUCH MORE IMPORTANT THAN WHAT YOU ACCUMULATE. They are of infinitely more value than is the grand total on your balance sheet. In fact, WHEN THESE THINGS ARE GOOD — IT DOESN'T MATTER WHETHER YOUR BALANCE SHEET EVEN BALANCES!

NOTES

[1] *The Evansville Courier* — Sunday, August 8, 1993, "Identifying And Buying The Right 'Toys' Can Be Serious Business" (Cox News Service).

[2] Terry Hershey, *Young Adult Ministry* (Loveland, CO: Group Books, 1986), 39.

[3] Tim Kimmel, *Little House on the Freeway* (Portland: Multnomah, 1987).

[4] Mignon McLaughlin, *The Neurotic's Notebook* (publication details unknown).

[5] "The Forgotten Four Hundred: Chicago's First Millionaires," *American Heritage,* November 1987, 37.

[6] Tom L. Eisenman, *Temptations Men Face: Straightforward Talk on Power, Money, Affairs, Perfectionism, Insensitivity* (Downers Grove, IL: InterVarsity Press) pp. 137-138.

CHAPTER EIGHT

My Daughter Married a Workaholic
EXODUS 18

STUDS TERKEL began his widely-acclaimed book entitled, *Working: People Talk About What They Do All Day and How They Feel About What They Do,* with the following observation:

> *"This book, being about work, is by its very nature, about violence — to the spirit as well as to the body. It is about ulcers as well as accidents. About shouting matches as well as fist fights. About nervous breakdowns as well as kicking the dog around. It is, above all (or beneath all), about daily humiliations."*[1]

It's sad, but true: Millions of Americans regard their work as something to endure. A pill to swallow. An onslaught through which to survive. James Russell Lowell called work, *"Something . . . which must be done, whether you like it or not."* Another man has dubbed it, *"drudgery in disguise."* Statistics tell us that only 1/10 of the American work force has even a moderate level of satisfaction with their jobs. The overwhelming majority finds work to be dull and meaningless.

In addition, Patterson and Kim in their study, *"The Day America Told the Truth,"* discovered that only one in four employees gives his or her best effort on the job, and that about 20% of the average worker's time is wasted.

Behind the Tent Flaps

And that's among those who actually do work. Charles Colson and Jack Eckerd, in their book, *Why America Doesn't Work,* maintain that the traditional American work ethic has its roots in religion, and as America has grown increasingly secularistic — work has died a thousand deaths. The authors point to the thousands of able-bodied men and women who live on government handouts — refusing to work because they're paid not to.

Then there's the flip-side. As epidemic as sloth is in our culture, as much hatred as we obviously express toward our work, overwork is just as prevalent. Our culture is besieged by workaholics and overachievers, who, in a mad pursuit for money, power, and fame frantically work themselves into heart attacks and nervous breakdowns, family disruptions, and even strokes. People who are so busy they never pause to enjoy life — never seem to have fun. "An idle mind" may very well be "the devil's workshop," but an overworked mind and body can lead to an early grave.

FOUR BIBLICALLY-BASED PRINCIPLES REGARDING WORK

And that's why, right at the outset of this chapter, I want to give you four biblically-based principles regarding work. Here's the first: **WORK IS A GIFT FROM GOD, NOT A CURSE.**

Work is not a sentence to be carried out, it is not a penance to be paid. On the contrary, when we open our Bibles to Genesis 1, we find that WORK is the first verb of life, **"In the beginning, God CREATED."** At the inception of history, God is found working.

Then in chapter 2, when God made man, He . . .

". . . formed the man from the dust of the ground and breathed into his nostrils the breath of life, and the man became a living being" (Gen 2:7).

Then He . . .

My Daughter Married a Workaholic

". . . took the man and put him in the Garden of Eden to work it and take care of it" (Gen 2:15).

That was Adam's assigned duties. He was to work the Garden and take care of it. Which should settle forever the argument as to which is the oldest profession: *It's landscaping, what else?*

I love the story about the argument between a farmer, an engineer and a politician as to the oldest profession on earth. The farmer said,

"My profession is the oldest, because Adam was a tiller of the soil."

But the engineer said, *"No, my profession is the oldest, because before man was God. And God was obviously an engineer, because he created the world out of total chaos."*

To which the politician replied, *"And where do you think all that chaos came from?"*

Isn't that incredible? The first thing God did with man was give him a job! And please understand, Adam's job was given BEFORE he sinned, not after, settling forever the thought that work is a curse. The curse that came from man's sin was a curse on the ground, so that it wouldn't be as responsive as it once had been, and man would now have to sweat it out in order to make the ground bring forth its harvest. But the labor itself was a gift. Given, not by clenched fists, but by tender hands. *Child of God, the thing that you do for at least 40% of your waking hours is a high and holy function.* It is the most dignified expression of life and you ought to be proud of that thing you do. Whatever it may be!

And the fact that God is still at work — sustaining the world, and restraining evil and saving mankind —gives even more legitimacy to your efforts. Jesus said, **"My Father is always at his work to this very day, and I, too, am working"** (John 5:17). Paul, writing to the Thessalonians, said that **"if a man will not work, he shall not eat"** (2 Thess 3:10). He added that if a man refuses to provide for his family, **"he has denied the faith and is worse than an unbeliever"** (1 Tim 5:8). And he warned not just against personal idleness, but also **"to keep away from every brother who is idle"** (2 Thess 3:6).

The point is well-taken. *Your work matters to God.* And as long as you are physically able, you are to be about the business of work. In fact, as a Christian, you are to be the most diligent, most responsible, most thorough, most loyal employee that can be found.

Which brings us to a second principle: **LAZINESS IS A SIN, NOT A VIRTUE.**

In fact, at the end of the sixth century, Pope Gregory the Great called laziness one of *"the seven deadly sins."* Solomon agreed. In his book of Proverbs, Solomon gives plenty of air time to those he calls, **"sluggards."** And he gives us at least four clues as the character of one who will not work.

First, he says that *The Lazy Person Has Trouble Getting Started.* Proverbs 6:9 says, **"How long will you lie there, you sluggard? When will you get up from your sleep?"** Proverbs 26:14 adds, **"As a door turns on its hinges, so a sluggard turns on his bed."**

Isn't that graphic? The alarm sounds, but the sluggard shifts and rolls, shouting to the ceiling, *"I'll get going soon! Give me five more minutes!"*

There's a story about a fellow who was employed by a duke and duchess in Europe.

> *"James,"* said the duchess to this employee, *"How long have you been with us?"*
> *"About thirty years,"* he replied.
> *"According to my records,"* said the duchess, *"you were employed to look after the dog."*
> *"Yes, Ma'am,"* James replied.
> *"James, that dog died twenty-seven years ago."*
> *"Yes, ma'am,"* he said. *"What would you like me to do now?"*

That's the lazy man. He has a hard time getting motivated.

Second, *The Lazy Person Seldom Finishes What He Has*

Started. Proverbs 12:27 says, **"The lazy man does not roast his game, but the diligent man prizes his possessions."** (*I like to catch fish, but I don't like to clean them.* That's the thought.) In Ecclesiastes, Solomon wrote, **"If a man is lazy, the rafters sag; if his hands are idle, the house leaks."** In the house of a lazy man, there are all sorts of unfinished projects. He'll get around to them — someday!

Third, *The Lazy Person Is Always Armed With Excuses*. Proverbs 22:13 says, **"The sluggard says, 'There is a lion outside!' or, 'I will be murdered in the streets!'"** Or, *the pollen count is too high today.* Or, *I have a cold!* Or, *it's raining!* To the lazy man, there's always a reason why *now* isn't a good time.

Fourth, *The Lazy Man Is Always Down On His Luck*. Proverbs 15:19 says, **"The way of the sluggard is blocked with thorns, but the path of the upright is a highway."** Everybody has a streak of bad luck from time to time, but Solomon is referring to the guy who is *always* in a pickle. He thinks it's bad luck; Solomon says it's blatant irresponsibility.

Contrary to what you may hear on the streets — laziness is not a virtue. And parents, if you have a sluggard in the making — if you have a child in your home that seems more than content to sit in front of Sega and vegetate alongside the kids from *Saved By The Bell* — you need to deal with that. And the earlier you set the patterns, the deeper they will be seated in your child's heart. He needs to know — and know it from you — that a smart man is not one who gets *out* of a job — but one who knows the true value and delight of honest, hard work. I am so thankful for parents who taught me that. Who taught me to finish mowing the lawn and then go play ball. Who taught me to get to work on time even if it meant riding my bike in the rain. Who said, *"Sure you can go on that school trip to Washington, D. C. But you're gonna have to earn the money."*

The old Jewish rabbis used to say, *"He who does not teach his child a trade teaches him to be a thief."* Now that may sound archaic in the hip-hopping 1990's, but it's still very sage advice indeed.

Which brings me to Principle #3: **HARD WORK IS A THING OF HONOR, NOT A REASON FOR REBUKE.**

Proverbs 10:4: **"Lazy hands make a man poor, but diligent hands bring wealth."** Paul told the Thessalonians to **"settle down and earn the bread they eat"** (2 Thess 3:12b).

I don't know what it is, but there's something about hard work and joy — they just seem to go together! I love the words of Vince Lombardi, the legendary coach of the Green Bay Packers: *"I firmly believe that man's finest hour, his greatest fulfillment to all he holds dear, is that moment when he has worked his heart out in a good cause and lies exhausted on the field of battle victorious."*

The happiest people I know are those who have striven for something worthwhile and won. There's a sense of accomplishment and fulfillment that cannot be matched, when, after the training and straining and wheeling and dealing and sweating and achieving and growing and working it's done!

You know what the best-selling T-shirt in Japan was in 1991? You know what message was emblazoned across the front? In large block letters, it announced, *"We're Number One!"* You know what the best selling T-shirt was, that same year, in the United States? *"Bart Simpson, Underachiever and Proud of it."*

Sorry. I don't buy it. In my experience, I have never met a proud underachiever. Because we're not wired that way. We've been made in the image of our Creator, Who, after forming the world in six days, paused, sucked in His breath and said, *"It is very good."* Work is not a drudgery to avoid; it is a thing of beauty and joy!

Mark Twain said it best. He said he hadn't done *"a lick of work"* in over fifty years. He wrote, *"I have always been able to gain my living without doing any work; for the writing of books and magazine matter was always play, not work. I enjoyed it; it was merely billiards to me."*

There are three qualities which should mark the work of every believer. And I base these qualities on two passages in the

New Testament. First, in Colossians 3:23, which says: **"Whatever you do, work at it with all your heart, as working for the Lord, not for men."** And also, Romans 12:11, which says, **"Never be lacking in zeal, but keep your spiritual fervor, serving the Lord."**

First, your work is to be marked by HIGH ENERGY.

"Never be lacking in zeal," says Paul.

Second, your work is to be marked by HEALTHY ENTHUSIASM. **"Work at it with all your heart."** Whether you're in a visible role, or an invisible role . . . whether you are highly acclaimed or scornfully shunned — do it with fervor. Walt Frazier, former teammate of the great Willis Reed, captain of the champion New York Knicks teams of the early seventies, said, *"No one ever out-hustled Willis. At practice, during a game, or even at a kids' clinic. What did it for him was desire. As a player and a man, he was always on fire."*

Third, your work is to be marked by WHOLEHEARTED EXCELLENCE.

"Work at it with all your heart," says Paul, **"as working for the Lord, not for men"** (Col 3:23). And work that is done unto the Lord is work that is done well. It's not shoddy, it's not half-done, it's not slapped together at the last minute — work offered to the Lord is *always* top-drawer. Always.

An old legend says that over the carpenter shop in Nazareth Jesus had a sign that read, *"My yoke is easy — it fits."* Now I don't know about that, but can you imagine Jesus producing a shoddy chair or doing a half-way job on someone's kitchen cabinets? NO! In fact, in the book of Mark, when the people of Nazareth heard Jesus preaching, they said, **"Isn't He the carpenter?"** (Mark 6:3). Not *a* carpenter; not one among many. But THE carpenter. I'm convinced that Jesus was a master craftsman, driven by high energy, healthy enthusiasm, and a wholehearted drive for excellence.

Having said that, there's a fourth principle, which brings us to the meat of this chapter. Are you ready? **WORKAHOLISM**

IS A MORAL DEFECT, NOT JUST A HARMLESS QUIRK.

Yes, work, in and of itself, is good. In fact, *very* good. And hard, challenging, even reasonably stressful work is one of the great thrills of life. *But consuming work?* The kind of work that ravenously devours health, family, and spiritual fervor? That's wrong. Dead wrong. And when you can't stop, even though you want to, or when you stay at the office, feeling guilty for knocking off as long as anyone else is still at his post — that's workaholism. And it is a sin.

The tragedy is, most WORKAHOLICS work, not so much for the money, but to PROVE SOMETHING. They slave away, trying to BE SOMEBODY. To prove to his father that he really could amount to something. The workaholic desperately needs the affirmation of others, because his perfectionistic bent refuses to allow him to affirm himself. And so he finds all kinds of surface reasons for why he has to work overtime — or why he can't take a vacation — when it really is nothing more than an inner compulsion to prove that he really is a person of value.

Some WORKAHOLICS work because they're gripped by feelings of indispensability. *"If I don't do it, it won't get done. If I'm not here to make things happen — things won't happen. I'm the vital cog! I'm the key to our success!"*

Still others can't seem to distinguish between ACTIVITY and ACCOMPLISHMENT. Talk about active! Such people never quit! But what's being accomplished? They're knocking themselves out — but for what? There have been times in my life when I've done that. And yet, looking back, they were my least productive times.

Other workaholics work to escape PROBLEMS they cannot seem to solve. Sometimes the workaholic pores over his desk — because he's more secure behind that desk than he is at home with a wife who is hurting, children who need him, or a spiritual problem that desperately needs his attention.

Yet others work because they're blatantly unwilling to DELEGATE. *"No one else can do it quite like I can do it."*

ANOTHER PEEK BEHIND THE FLAPS

Which brings us, once again, to the tent flaps of one of the great heroes of Scripture, a man who also happened to be an admitted workaholic. I refer to Moses, the leader of the Exodus. The one who marched into Pharaoh's court and demanded the freedom of his people. The one who led two million Israelites right through the mouth of the Red Sea. The one who led Israel's army into victory after victory on the battlefield. And now, also the one who handled all of Israel's personal and legal squabbles.

That's right. Whenever any two of the more than two million Jews had a personal problem, they brought it to Moses to solve. And Moses learned early on that you just can't wave a rod and make *"people problems"* go away. No, people problems are a whole lot tougher than Red Sea problems. People problems require careful and painstaking interaction and counseling. And as far as Moses was concerned — HE WAS THE ONLY ONE WHO COULD HANDLE IT.

Which is why his father-in-law came to see him one day. At least that was one of the reasons. The other reason Jethro came to Moses was to reunite Moses with his family.

> **"Jethro, Moses' father-in-law, together with Moses' sons and wife, came to him in the desert, where he was camped near the mountain of God"** (Exod 18:5).

You may remember that Zipporah, having circumcised her son in order to save her husband's life — had taken the boys and gone back to live with Daddy. She was angry, so she went home to Daddy. But thank the Lord, Jethro was a man of integrity. He knew that Zipporah belonged with her husband, so he refused to allow her to stay indefinitely and came instead to restore to Moses his family. I point that out because you need to know that Jethro has no axe to grind. His later rebuke of Moses is not some subtle attempt to vindicate his position all along that Moses wasn't good enough for little Zippy. No, Jethro was staunchly committed to the health and stability of his daughter's marriage. Which means he was also committed to a loving, affirming relationship with his son-in-law. *How do I know that?* Well, when . . .

> "Moses told his father-in-law about everything the LORD had done to Pharaoh and the Egyptians for Israel's sake and about all the hardships they had met along the way and how the LORD had saved them. Jethro was delighted to hear about all the good things the LORD had done for Israel in rescuing them from the hand of the Egyptians" (Exod 18:8-9).

In fact . . .

> "Jethro, Moses' father-in-law, brought a burnt offering and other sacrifices to God, and Aaron came with all the elders of Israel to eat bread with Moses' father-in-law in the presence of God" (Exod 18:12).

And it was in that context of affirmation and celebration that Jethro noticed something. Something he knew spelled trouble.

> "The next day Moses took his seat to serve as judge for the people, and they stood around him from morning till evening" (Exod 18:13).

That's all you have to read, folks, to know that Moses was overcommitted. **"From morning till evening."** And Jethro watched throughout the day, observing that line growing longer and longer. He also noted a battle-weary Moses slump into his tent and tumble onto his La-Z-Boy mat long after dark. Then he listened as Moses, totally spent emotionally, began to gripe at the kids and grumble at his wife. He noticed the economy-sized bottle of Mylanta on the coffee table and decided something had to be said. You know how in-laws are. They can't keep quiet about anything. So he said . . .

> "What is this you are doing for the people? Why do you alone sit as judge, while all these people stand around you from morning till evening?" (Exod 18:14).

Talk about on target! Jethro asked two vital questions: 1] *"What is this you are doing?"* and, 2] *"Why are you doing it alone?"*

The first question related to priorities, the second to personnel. *"Moses, look at how you're spending your time! You've got longer lines than Disneyland! You're supposed to be leading this nation, man, yet all you're doing is refereeing petty squabbles! Why are you trying to do this all alone?"*

By the way, you need to ask yourself those questions occasionally. You need to stick it in PARK, get alone, and say, *"What am I doing with my time? Are the priorities I say are priorities, really priorities?"* That is, *"Can I tell that they are priorities by the way I invest my time?"* And second, *"Can't some of this burden be shifted to someone else? Not because I'm lazy, but because the load is more than one person can handle."*

Now I'm impressed that Moses doesn't respond with anger — he doesn't offer excuses — he just says:

> **"Moses answered him, 'Because the people come to me to seek God's will. Whenever they have a dispute, it is brought to me, and I decide between the parties and inform them of God's decrees and laws'"** (Exod 18:15-16).

"Jethro, I know this is a big job. And yes, I AM tired. But Jethro, if I don't do it, it's not going to get done!" Ah, the favorite ten words of the workaholic. Moses says, *"They come to me to find out God's will. Who else could do that but me?"*

Now if I had been in Jethro's sandals, I probably would have said, *"Gee, Moses, you're right. This is a big job. I'm sorry I said anything. Hey, hang in there, bud."* Not Jethro. He said:

> **"What you are doing is not good"** (Exod 18:17b).

Now remember, he's talking to God's handpicked leader! The man who held the rod! Who struck the rock and brought them through the Sea! Yet Jethro says, *"Hey man, this isn't good!"* Then he explains why . . .

> **"You and these people who come to you will only wear yourselves out"** (Exod 18:18a).

That's not just a reason, that's a warning. *"Moses, you keep this up and you're going to burn out!"*

> **"The work is too heavy for you; you cannot handle it alone"** (Exod 18:18b).

Behind the Tent Flaps

Now honestly, I'm not convinced that I'm the one who should deal with this topic. After all, ten days ago my accountability group stomped all over me for, you guessed, it, trying to do too much. This past Wednesday I visited a friend in the hospital, who introduced me to her friend, by saying, *"This is Steve Wyatt. He's a workaholic, too."* And yet here I am writing this stuff as though I was some kind of expert? I mean, *Who am I to tell anyone to stop trying to cover all the bases?*

But what was so wonderful about Jethro's rebuke is that he offered more than a warning — he also offered solid, helpful advice.

> **"Listen now to me and I will give you some advice, and may God be with you. You must be the people's representative before God and bring their disputes to him. Teach them the decrees and laws, and show them the way to live and the duties they are to perform"** (Exod 18:19-20).

Moses, you need to change your methodology. You've got to stop trying to meet needs one person at a time. You need to develop a public teaching ministry. That's my need, too. I am called of God to teach Scripture in a relevant, accurate manner so that the people whom God has entrusted to my care will get the counsel they need. There's no way that I can counsel 2300 people every week. But I can teach. And when the pulpit I fill is marked by careful, considered, compassionate counsel — the Body is strengthened and my work is accomplished. And some of the other work that needs done? It just has to be done by others, that's all there is to it! In fact, that's Jethro's second piece of advice.

> **"But select capable men from all the people —men who fear God, trustworthy men who hate dishonest gain —and appoint them as officials over thousands, hundreds, fifties and tens. Have them serve as judges for the people at all times, but have them bring every difficult case to you; the simple cases they can decide themselves. That will make your load lighter, because they will share it with you"** (Exod 18:21-22).

You mark that verse, you who are hard-driving overachievers. God actually wants your load to be *lighter*. I realize that you might need to read that verse again. More slowly. After all, most Christians think that bleary-eyed busyness is THE badge of spiritual honor! That bags under your eyes and sagging shoulders are an irrefutable sign that you're really giving it up for God! When that's not to be the case at all!

> "Moses listened to his father-in-law and did everything he said. He chose capable men from all Israel and made them leaders of the people, officials over thousands, hundreds, fifties and tens. They served as judges for the people at all times. The difficult cases they brought to Moses, but the simple ones they decided themselves" (Exod 18:24-26).

And as a result, do you know happened among those people? FOUR THINGS . . .

First, Moses was able to concentrate on his primary gift and calling, by focusing his energies on his teaching ministry . . .

Second, new leadership was developed . . .

Third, the people's problems were resolved more swiftly, and harmony was restored in the ranks . . .

And finally, little Gershom and his brother got their daddy back, "Zippy" had a husband again, and Jethro returned to Midian a happy man.

A WORKABLE PLAN FOR RECOVERY

I wonder, am I writing to a modern-day Moses right now? Could it be that there are more than just a few workaholics out there? If so, I've got a message from the Lord for you. Now I'm not the most qualified person to say these things — but hey, it's my job. So here goes. I want to offer you a balanced, workable plan for recovery. But understand: you won't listen to a word I say unless you're convinced you need to hear it. My accountability group really nailed me — but the reason why is because I'd had enough. In the same way, Moses listened because there comes a time when you're weary enough to try anything!

So how about it? *HAVE YOU HAD ENOUGH?* Here are a few questions you can ask to find out if perhaps you, too, are right on the verge of a breakdown. *Here's how you can know when you've had enough:*

- You know you have enough health insurance if the only way you can make ends meet is to break a major bone every month and have brain surgery once a year.
- You know your dogs have barked enough when the neighbors chip in to buy an army surplus bazooka, and take turns standing guard at your back fence.
- You know you've been married long enough if you accidentally drive off and leave your wife in a truck stop but keep driving anyway.
- You know you've been single long enough if your idea of a big Saturday night is comparing brands of soap with the women in the laundry room.
- You know you've eaten enough peanut butter and jelly sandwiches if you can't drive anywhere without sticking to the roof of your car.
- You know you've had enough Chinese hot mustard when you breathe on your Moo Goo Gai Pan and it bursts into flame.
- You know you've been on the phone long enough when the operator asks you to deposit your Toyota.
- You know your stereo is loud enough when the University of California calls long distance and says you're registering nine on the Richter scale.
- You know you've been at the party long enough when the hostess walks in wearing curlers and asks you to empty the trash cans and put out the cat.

Well? *Have you had enough?* Are you tired of doing nothing but work? Are you weary of the feeling that if you don't do it, it won't get done? Are you sick of finding that your sense of value and worth is only measured by what you do at the office? Are you tired of seeing that sad look in your kids' eyes when you head out for yet another work-filled Saturday?

My Daughter Married a Workaholic

I know, it's only temporary. It's *always* "only temporary." Next quarter will be better. In another year, the business will be stable, and you'll have more than enough time to kick back and relax. I know. I've said the same thing. "Honey, next month will be less hectic." For years I told Vanessa there was light at the end of the tunnel. And yet what I found was the light at the end of the tunnel was really the headlamp of another oncoming train! And so I lived life in the fast lane, lacking the necessary discipline to limit my entanglements, and choosing instead to be dominated by my work. And in the process, I sacrificed the relationships of life that really matter.

Now if you're ready to admit that it's not going to be any better next month — or even the next — take a look at these four suggestions.

First, if you would break your addiction to work, you must **REASSESS YOUR SCHEDULE**.

There are limits to what one person can do. Besides, every time-management study I know reveals that work always expands to fill available time. That is, if you plan a two-hour meeting, that's how long it'll take, even though the agenda might only require 45 minutes. Experts tell us that when working late is the habit, you tend to slack off. You know there's no rush, so you're not as focused and don't push yourself as hard. You also waste time on things that don't need done, or you socialize in the hall. And though you work later, it's not necessarily because of the amount of work, but because you had it in your mind that you were *going* to work late. The result is — we often convince ourselves that we need to work all those hours, when we don't.

It used to be that working late was considered heroic and the sign of a person on his way up. But no more. *"In the last two and a half years we've seen a dramatic change,"* says Dan Stamp, a time-management specialist. *"Now it is mainstream thinking that there has to be more to life than just work.... I think the people who reject long hours will be the real leaders in the years to come — they're the brightest, the innovators. The guys logging really long hours aren't seen as heroes anymore. They're seen as turkeys."*

Jesus knew the value of taking time off. Many was the time He'd grab His men and head for the hills. Even though the needs remained and the press of humanity never ceased. But you see, Jesus knew when enough was enough. He knew that if you burn the candle at both ends — you'll end up a frazzled mess.

So I challenge you: Take a break. Forget for 24 hours that you're a cop, or an engineer, or an attorney. Find some tree and take a nap under its branches. Take a walk along the river. Spend an evening with a friend. Take your mate to dinner. If God took time to rest, don't kid yourself into thinking you don't need to.

Or why not decide that this week you're going to leave the office an hour earlier than usual — no matter what. I guarantee that you will get the same amount of work done as when you worked the extra hour. Put it to the test. See if I'm right.

But you won't do that, I'm convinced, unless you're willing to take step #2 as well: **YOU MUST ALSO REDEFINE SUCCESS.**

I find that most workaholics have a very distorted view of success. They pursue a far less noble goal: They're out to make a living, when they ought to be building a life. The great irony of much of what passes for success is that although you have more money to buy more things — you have no time to play with those things.

Pollster Lou Harris tells us that the average person has 32% less leisure time than he did a decade ago. As a result, that dream car has been parked so long that it's used more air in the tires than it has gas in the tank. The country house for weekend getaways may as well be in another country. The two-week ski trip to Vail has been delayed for the third straight winter. And the treasured wooden skiff hasn't touched anything wet in eight months. Blessed are the toys for they shall inherit . . . dust!

And it's not just material things; personal lives also suffer due to this mangled view of success. Let's face it: you can't spend 60 hours a week as a saber-toothed tiger, then walk in the front door as tame as a pussy cat. It's very tough to burn yourself out for 12 hours a day and still be fired up when you get home.

Peter Lynch, the famous Wall Street broker, stated that he had spent all of his waking hours *"poring over company balance sheets and meeting with executives to try to find the next hot stock. I didn't have time to watch sports or look at newspapers and read only about one book a year. Worse still, my family had become strangers."*

And you call that, "SUCCESS?"

James Dobson writes,

> *In twentieth-century America, it is almost inevitable that a vigorous competition arises between a man's job and his home. Achieving a balance between two areas of responsibility requires constant vigilance, and, quite frankly, most men tip the scales dramatically in the direction of their employment.*[2]

And yet, I have never heard a businessman, at the end of his career say, *"You know, if I had it to do all over again, I'd spend more time at the office. I'd get up earlier and work harder and stay longer."* NO. But I have heard many a man say, *"If I had it do over, I'd spend more time with my family. I'd get to know my kids better. I'd even spend time with my wife."* And the irony is some experts tell us that if you spend more time with your family, you're more likely to go further in your career. WHY? Because there would be less fights, fewer conflicts. I know that's true for me. I have never, in the 21+ years of our marriage — never lost a day's work worrying about some major blow-up at home. And just knowing that things were right at home has freed my mind for creativity and leadership and a lavish investment while I'm on the job.

Step #3 has to do with **BALANCE**. The key to recovery is found in striking that all-important, but very delicate, balance. Working hard, but not making work your god. Giving your best, but refusing to so wrap your self-esteem in your job — that if the company folds, or if you get laid off — your very reason for living is cut out from beneath you. Be diligent, but don't neglect your family. Grind it out, but save some in reserve for investment in the kingdom.

Sandy Mobley was working 70 to 80 hours a week (including weekends) with lots of travel. She said, *"I never had time for myself. I had no social life to speak of and was quickly reaching the point of burnout. I was tired all the time and feeling sluggish and putting on weight because I had no time to work out."* Over a period of time and with a job change she cut back to 40- or 45-hour weeks with minimal travel. The change has been dramatic. She says, *"I am feeling great. Everything has picked up. I have time for friends, exercise, little projects. And I am actually getting more work done with more quality and creativity."*

That's not so hard to believe. Because when you're tired, you work slower, you don't think as clearly, you're less creative, and you make more mistakes. You get home exhausted, but it's difficult to sleep because your mind is still racing. You wake up the next morning tired, and the cycle continues. Obviously, all of us have to work late sometime. But a steady diet of long hours kills creativity, energy and enthusiasm, and the resulting stress can eventually kill you. There's got to be a balance. *Is it easy to find?* NO. Is it worth the search? No doubt about it.

Then finally, step #4, if you want to get a grip on work — **YOU MUST REALIZE WHO IT IS YOU'RE *REALLY* WORKING FOR.**

You need to remember — in that moment when the rush of adrenalin is flowing, when your heart quickens from the scent of a deal, when your head pulsates with the thrill of the chase — remember, YOUR WORK IS A HOLY VOCATION. The thing you do — your work — is a drink offering to the Lord. There is no such thing as a sacred job and a secular job. If you are a believer — your work is for His glory, not your own benefit.

Scripture says,

> **"Whether you eat or drink or whatever you do, do it all for the glory of God"** (1 Cor 10:31).
>
> **"And whatever you do, whether in word or deed, do it all in the name of the LORD Jesus, giving thanks to God the Father through him"** (Col 3:17).
>
> **"Whatever you do, work at it with all your heart, as working for the LORD, not for men. It is the LORD Christ you are serving"** (Col 3:23-24).

That means, housewife, when you a cook a meal, you cook that meal as if Jesus were going to eat it. You clean that house as if the Lord were your next guest. Teachers, educate your students as if Jesus were at one of those desks. Attorneys, fight for the truth as if Jesus were your client. Doctors . . . Nurses, care for your patients as though the very Son of God was on that bed. Salesmen, pitch your product as if Jesus were your customer. Businessmen, treat your clients as if they were the Lord. Accountants, audit your books . . . Secretaries, type and file . . . Managers, lead and plan . . . as if what you are doing is done unto Him. BECAUSE, MY FRIEND, THAT IS IN FACT WHAT YOU ARE DOING! Christian, you don't work just to earn a living, and you certainly don't work to substantiate your worth — you work as unto the Lord.

To understand that is to stop frantically trying to find the pot at the end of the rainbow or climb to the top of the corporate ladder. But instead, by whatever means — by word or by deed — Christ is honored by your efforts.

NOTES

[1] Studs Terkel, *Working: People Talk About What They Do All Day and How They Feel About What They Do* (New York: Pantheon Books), p. xi.

[2] James Dobson, *Straight Talk to Men and Their Wives,* p. 129.

CHAPTER NINE

When You've Married a Short Fuse
1 SAMUEL 25

Are you married to a short fuse?

Is the home where you live a home scarred by uncontrolled rage and seething hostility?

If so, perhaps the biblical story recorded for us in 1 Samuel 25 will be of some help to you. It's a story of one of the lesser lights of Scripture to be sure — a story not often listed among the Top Ten favorites of the Christian church — but I find it strikingly relevant and packed with meaning. So let's pull back the tent flaps and, perhaps for some, for the very first time, discover together the story of Abigail and Nabal.

THE PRINCIPALS

There are three principal characters in this story.

According to Samuel, the first of these characters is DAVID, the king-elect of Israel. We read:

> "Now Samuel died, and all Israel assembled and mourned for him; and they buried him at his home in Ramah. Then David moved down into the Desert of Maon" (1 Sam 25:1).

In other words, David was a fugitive in his own country. King

Behind the Tent Flaps

Saul still occupied the throne, and although David had slain the giant, had been anointed by Samuel, and was obviously more beloved in the hearts of the people than Saul — David's life was in jeopardy. Saul wanted him dead. So he's living in the desert as a fugitive; he's hiding in caves, eating what he could find, sleeping where he could lie.

And not just David. By the time we come to 1 Samuel 25, some 600 men had joined his entourage. Some were political malcontents, others were running from bad debts — and so they came to join ranks with David. In years to come these would become David's inner circle, his warriors, his most trusted advisors. But now — they were merely hungry mouths to feed. And so, in order to provide for their necessary sustenance, David and his men began providing a service to the many shepherds and ranchers whose flocks and herds grazed the fields of the desert.

But more on that later. The second principal character is **NABAL.**

> **"A certain man in Maon, who had property there at Carmel, was very wealthy. He had a thousand goats and three thousand sheep, which he was shearing in Carmel. His name was Nabal"** (1 Sam 25:2-3a).

In those days, a man's name reflected his character. It revealed the kind of person that he was. Nabal means, *"fool."* And his name fit, quite frankly. Nabal was a tough-hearted, bigoted, stubborn, prejudiced fool. Not only that, but he was **"surly and mean in his dealings"** (1 Sam 25:3b).

When you want to really know the truth about a man, just ask his employees. What did Nabal's employees think about him? They said, **"He is such a wicked man that no one can talk to him"** (1 Sam 25:17b).

It has been said,

> *"A fool who knows his foolishness is wise; but a fool who thinks himself wise, he is a fool indeed."*[m]

Well, Nabal was a "fool indeed." He was so evil, so headstrong, so self-willed you couldn't even reason with the man. You couldn't hold an intelligent conversation with him because he was the one with the facts. He was coarse. Feisty. Rich. Opinionated. Egocentric. Hot-tempered. I guess the best way to put it is that Nabal was sort of a combination between Saddam Hussein, Ebenezer Scrooge, and ??? [you fill it in].

Unfortunately, even a jerk like Nabal often gets married. And, unfortunately for her, Nabal's wife, Abigail, grabbed the short straw. Ironically, Abigail was an exceptionally wonderful person. 1 Samuel describes her as **"an intelligent and beautiful woman"** (1 Sam 25:3b).

What a combination! She was intelligent — discerning, bright, an extremely thoughtful woman. She planned her work in advance, she seemed well-prepared for any unforeseen eventuality — in other words, she was a class act. And on top of that? She was a knockout! Listen, when Scripture says that a woman was beautiful, you'd better believe she was drop-dead gorgeous!

And as we'll see in a moment — Abigail used her beauty *and* her intellect, not only to intervene on behalf of her hot-tempered husband, but to stop the king-elect from making a very foolish choice.

The point I can't help but ponder is this: *How could a wonderful woman like Abigail wind up married to a jerk like Nabal? Really!* He was a dud; she, on the other hand, was a catch. All he had going for him was a pocketful of money; she had everything going for her.

But you see, in those days a woman didn't choose her own mate. She had to take whomever Daddy said she was to take. That's why this classy lady is now married to a man in love with himself and his money. A man who loved drinking and carousing, a man who came home at night bloodied and scarred, cursing and swearing and kicking the dog. And that wasn't what Abigail was about at all.

Unfortunately, such painful unions still take place. Even in a day when we choose our own poison (so to speak) — we often make the wrong choice. And if the truth were known, maybe that's how you feel. You married a loser, and are convinced that you have made the most horrible mistake of your life. Or maybe you thought your mate was different than he has turned out. Maybe it was only after the wedding that he began to show his true colors. Whatever, you find yourself living daily with an angry, hostile, stubborn man or woman. *How should you handle such a disappointing reality?* Well, let me show you how Abigail handled it.

THE PLOT

"While David was in the desert, he heard that Nabal was shearing sheep" (1 Sam 25:4).

You're thinking, *"Big deal."* It WAS a big deal . . . to David. Because he and his men had voluntarily protected Nabal's sheep as they grazed along the hillsides of Maon. They kept marauding hill people and tribesmen from invading his flocks and carrying away his profits. And although they hadn't signed any contracts, although no formal agreement had been reached — there was an informal gentlemen's agreement between David and all of the ranchers in the region that when it came time to shear the sheep — David would receive remuneration for services rendered.

Don't forget, David has been on the run for years. No doubt he is exhausted, tired of sleeping on the ground, and could really use a bath; and now, on top of all that, the troops are getting hungry. The food supply is nearly gone. So he's thrilled to hear that Nabal is shearing sheep, because that means payday is just around the corner.

In case you're wondering whether David's men really performed this service, take a look at verse 15. One of Nabal's servants reports:

"These men were very good to us. They did not mistreat us, and the whole time we were out in the fields near them nothing was missing. Night and day they were a wall around us all the time we were herding our sheep near them" (1 Sam 25:15-16).

When You've Married a Short Fuse

In other words, they did their job! All they want now is their well-deserved pay.

> "So he [David] **sent ten young men and said to them, 'Go up to Nabal at Carmel and greet him in my name. Say to him: 'Long life to you! Good health to you and your household! And good health to all that is yours! Now I hear that it is sheep-shearing time. When your shepherds were with us, we did not mistreat them, and the whole time they were at Carmel nothing of theirs was missing. Ask your own servants and they will tell you. Therefore be favorable toward my young men, since we come at a festive time. Please give your servants and your son David whatever you can find for them'"** (1 Sam 25:5-8).

There's no set fee. No demand for a socially acceptable 15% gratuity. Just *"whatever"* you want to give. And I'm convinced he fully expected Nabal to fulfill his end of the bargain. After all, he only sent 10 men, right? He could have sent 110 men. Or more. Now remember the servant's testimony. David and his men had carefully done their job. Not one among all of Nabal's flock was missing. And yet . . .

> **"When David's men arrived, they gave Nabal this message in David's name. Then they waited"** (1 Sam 25:9).

They weren't demanding. They weren't impatient. They quietly waited for Nabal to make the necessary arrangements.

They didn't have to wait long!

> **"Nabal answered David's servants, 'Who is this David? Who is this son of Jesse? Many servants are breaking away from their masters these days. Why should I take my bread and water, and the meat I have slaughtered for my shearers, and give it to men coming from who knows where?'"** (1 Sam 25:10-11).

Jerk! I mean, really! What a stupid, stingy, slime-ball. He's got more money than he could ever spend, and yet when it comes time to pay a man who rendered an invaluable service protecting his flocks and his herds — NABAL STIFFS THE GUY!

Behind the Tent Flaps

"David's men turned around and went back. When they arrived, they reported every word" (1 Sam 25:12).

How did David respond? Well, you've got to know that while they were gone, David had been getting the grill warmed up — he'd been toasting the buns and setting the table. This guy is hungry! More than ready to feast on the rewards of his labor! And when these ten men told him that there would be no feast, David said, **"Put on your swords!"** (1 Sam 25:13a). I know, that's a pretty strong reaction. And no, I'm not going to try to defend it.

But the fact is, this same scene is replayed in homes all across this country as husbands and wives — tired of the abuse, wearied by the constant tension — throw down the gauntlet and say, *"That's it! I've had it! I've put up with this long enough! This is the last straw! I'm not gonna take it anymore!"* And in that moment of rage, all sensibilities are lost, all restraint is gone.

Have you been there? In that moment when all hell breaks loose, you start devising the most damnable scheme, the most insane plan — and in that moment of rage, you're loaded for bear — and if doing the plan ruins you in the process? *"I don't care! I've had it!"*

That's where David was. Acting completely out of character, David launched what could prove to be the most self-destructive move of his life! *Thank goodness for Abigail.*

Just picture the scene: Four hundred angry fugitives are headed for Carmel. Meanwhile, back at the ranch, one of Nabal's servants heard what was about to happen and rushed to Abigail with this message:

> **"'David sent messengers from the desert to give our master his greetings, but he hurled insults at them. Yet these men were very good to us. They did not mistreat us, and the whole time we were out in the fields near them nothing was missing. Night and day they were a wall around us all the time we were herding our sheep near them. Now think it over and see what you can do, because disaster is hanging over our master and his whole household'"** (1 Sam 25:14b-17a).

When You've Married a Short Fuse

THE PEACEMAKER

What does Abigail do? How does she choose to respond? Did she rush over to Nabal's office to talk it over with him? No way, José. No one, not even Abigail, was willing to take that kind of gamble. Remember his rep?

"He is such a wicked man that no one can talk to him" (1 Sam 25:17b).

There's no reasoning with this man! You might as well be talking to a brick wall!

I heard the story about a man who was driving along a country road one day. Suddenly, from around the curve just ahead of him, a car came lurching in his direction — on his side of the road! He slammed on his brakes, and as they swerved past each other, the woman driver in the other car, screamed at him: *"Pig, pig!"*

Furious, he shouted back, *"Sow! Sow!"*

Pleased at his quick retort, he drove around the curve and crashed right into a pig.

That's Nabal. Couldn't tell the man a thing.

Which is why Abigail didn't even consider discussing the matter with him. He had long before closed his wife's spirit. She instinctively knew that he would be of no help to her at all. I wonder, *does your mate have a closed spirit toward you?* And are you the one who closed it? What with those harsh, belittling comments you make? Or your scornful reactions to her opinions and feelings? Or your blatant inability to admit that sometimes you may just be wrong? Always making crude comments at her expense? Forcing her to do things that violate her morality? Treating her like dirt? Like some filthy piece of garbage?

Why no wonder she no longer responds to you. No wonder she never lets you see her cry. No wonder her face is like a stone. No, Abigail was not about to confront Nabal. I mean, what could she expect? AN APOLOGY? Excuse me: *NABALS DON'T APOLOGIZE!*

Behind the Tent Flaps

Never mind that those two simple words, *"I'm sorry"* had the potential to diffuse this entire scene! Never mind that David was a man after God's own heart and would have certainly relented in the face such a humble word. Nabals don't like humility. They can't handle the thought of lowering themselves like that. To Nabal, an apology is a sign of weakness.

Which is why Senator Bob Packwood, for example, although he grudgingly admitted that groping and fondling his female employees were, in fact, "unwelcome and insensitive" actions — obviously evaded the "sorry" word. And, until threatened with expulsion, firmly refused to resign.

Then there's New York's former chief judge Sol Wachtler, who, instead of apologizing for harassing a New York socialite and her teenage daughter, portrayed himself as a victim of drugs and alcohol.

Pete Rose, banned from baseball and booted out of a sure spot in the Hall of Fame because of a betting scandal, never did apologize to his fans.

Sad but true: SORRY isn't in the vocabulary of a NABAL.

Now if you're married to a Nabal, no further explanation is necessary. You know full well that there are things you never say to an angry fool. And so, realizing that this was one of those times to be silent — Abigail kept the matter to herself.

To her credit, I find no hint that she saw this as a chance to get rid of the slob. She doesn't even display enough hostility to agree with the servant. He provided her with a perfect opportunity to vent some rage. But she doesn't. She didn't say, *"You know, he is a jerk, isn't he?"* Instead, I picture her swallowing a silent scream — and then, without any further delay, ***she began to formulate a plan.*** And what a plan it was.

> **"Abigail lost no time. She took two hundred loaves of bread, two skins of wine, five dressed sheep, five seahs of roasted grain, a hundred cakes of raisins and two hundred cakes of pressed figs, and loaded them on donkeys. Then she told her servants, 'Go on ahead; I'll follow you.' But she did not tell her husband Nabal"** (1 Sam 25:18-19).

When You've Married a Short Fuse

You know why, don't you? Had she told him her plan, he would have scuttled the entire project. Fool that he was, Nabal would have seen such actions as a sign of weakness. And he would have absolutely cringed had he known his wife was out there doing his dirty business. So she didn't tell him.

Some people say Abigail was wrong. They say that she wasn't being submissive. She wasn't honoring her husband. But I think she did the right thing. I think she knew her husband better than any of us know him. And she realized that the only way she could save his neck was to keep him out of it. We'll say more about that later.

"As she came riding her donkey into a mountain ravine, there were David and his men descending toward her, and she met them" (1 Sam 25:20).

He with a sword in his hand, and she with a lamb chop in hers. Not to mention the bread, fruit, cakes, and wine. Hey, I guarantee you, David sheathed that sword in a flash. Little drips of saliva cascaded from his lips as Abigail fell on her face before him still clutching to that hauntingly delicious piece of meat.

"She fell at his feet and said: 'My lord, let the blame be on me alone. Please let your servant speak to you; hear what your servant has to say. May my lord pay no attention to that wicked man Nabal. He is just like his name —his name is Fool, and folly goes with him. But as for me, your servant, I did not see the men my master sent'" (1 Sam 25:24-25).

And don't you dare criticize her for saying that. Hey, it was the truth! And I find no hint that she said it in a slanderous, gossipy spirit. She's not being critical — she's being truthful! She knows he's wicked. She knows the truth of his character. After all, isn't she right now in harm's way, simply because he was such a turkey? Her motives were right, people! She's doing her very best to keep that turkey husband of hers from adorning David's table, sliced and diced, and ready to eat.

Submission doesn't mean you stick your head in the sand! Any more than it means that you must stick your brains in neutral! Listen to her appeal . . .

> "'Now since the LORD has kept you, my master, from bloodshed and from avenging yourself with your own hands, as surely as the LORD lives and as you live, may your enemies and all who intend to harm my master be like Nabal. And let this gift, which your servant has brought to my master, be given to the men who follow you'" (1 Sam 25:26-27).

Unlike her foolish husband, Abigail appeals to David with the deepest of respect. She says . . .

> "'Please forgive your servant's offense, for the LORD will certainly make a lasting dynasty for my master, because he fights the LORD's battles. Let no wrongdoing be found in you as long as you live. Even though someone is pursuing you to take your life, the life of my master will be bound securely in the bundle of the living by the LORD your God. But the lives of your enemies he will hurl away as from the pocket of a sling. When the LORD has done for my master every good thing he promised concerning him and has appointed him leader over Israel, my master will not have on his conscience the staggering burden of needless bloodshed or of having avenged himself'" (1 Sam 25:28-31a).

"David, you don't want this thing on your conscience when you become king. You kill my husband, and you'll never live it down. It will haunt you throughout your entire reign as king. Don't let this be found on your permanent record." David replied . . .

> "'Praise be to the LORD, the God of Israel, who has sent you today to meet me. May you be blessed for your good judgment and for keeping me from bloodshed this day and from avenging myself with my own hands. Otherwise, as surely as the LORD, the God of Israel, lives, who has kept me from harming you, if you had not come quickly to meet me, not one male belonging to Nabal would have been left alive by daybreak.'
> Then David accepted from her hand what she had brought him and said, 'Go home in peace. I have heard your words and granted your request'" (1 Sam 25:32-35).

That's what author Stephen Covey would call a win-win situation. Nabal won, because he got to keep his neck. Abigail won, because she earned the respect of the king-elect. And

David won, because he was spared from one of the most foolish mistakes of his life.[2] All because Abigail stood in the gap and did what to many was an absolutely unthinkable and unjustifiable deed.

Can you believe it? There are some who say, *"Well, she should've just let David slice him up!"* Which seems like a strange reaction for Christians.

Then there are others who say she should never have acted without her husband's permission. There's a Greek word for that kind of logic: *HOGWASH!* Listen, I find no place in Scripture where a godly wife is expected to be her husband's doormat. I find, quite to the contrary, that there is a big difference between being assertive and being aggressive. There's a big difference between being proactive and being argumentative.

Remember Edith Bunker? Her friend came to visit one day and said, *"Edith, of all the people I know, you're practically the only one who has a happy marriage."*

Edith said, *"Really? Me and Archie . . . oh, thank you."*

Her friend said, *"What's your secret, Edith?"*

Edith replied, *"Oh, I ain't got no secret. Archie and me still have our fights. Of course, we don't let them go on too long. Somebody always says 'I'm sorry.' And Archie always says, It's okay, Edith.'"*[3]

In her book, *Peace & Quiet [and other hazards]*, Ethel Barrett tells of the time her husband drew up five rules which she was expected to follow.

1. *I was never again to ask anyone, even a pastor or a Bible teacher, any question in my husband's presence. I was to wait until I got home and find out the answer from him.*
2. *I was to be in my husband's home at all times, and not leave it without his permission.*
3. *I was never to be out at night alone (except for choir practice, in which case, I should come straight home at a decent hour).*
4. *I was never to question my husband's wisdom or decisions in any matter whatsoever.*

Behind the Tent Flaps

5. I was to cease speaking publicly in the future; I was never to speak again on the platform.[4]

GAG! That's not biblical submission. That's high-handed domination! That's macho-minded control! And I'm convinced that if Abigail had followed such insanity — if she had knuckled under to such a woefully inaccurate view of submission — her husband, her children, her home, her financial security, and everything she knew and loved would have been destroyed and taken from her!

Others say she should have divorced the man. Just gotten out. It was an obviously ugly situation; surely God would understand! And I'm convinced that if Nabal had been physically abusive to her, she *would've* gotten out. And rightly so.

I do not believe that God would have you stay in a marriage where your face gets smashed. I don't believe for a moment that God has even the slightest regard for a man who hits his mate. And I think it's only right that if you're trapped in a marriage where you or your children are in physical jeopardy, you ought to protect yourself and get out.

There's a lot of debate about what Abigail should have done. *But you know what I think?* I think it's none of our business. I know from experience that the Christian woman who finds herself married to an angry fool lives in such a tenuous situation that often, not even her closest friends will understand why she does what she does. Or how it is that she can respond the way that she responds. Sometimes you can't explain what you know in your heart you have to do.

Meanwhile, back at the ranch:

"Abigail went to Nabal . . ." (1 Sam 25:36a).

No doubt to explain to him how she had saved his life, and how David would not be coming to kill him after all . . . *and what was her reward for such a courageous deed?*

"He was in the house holding a banquet like that of a king. He was in high spirits and very drunk. So she told him nothing until daybreak" (1 Sam 25:36b).

Once again this wise woman, realizing that now was not the time, held her tongue and went to bed. You don't argue with a fool, especially when he's drunk. So she turns in, pulls the covers over her face, and, like so many nights before, cries herself to sleep. *What a great woman!* Man! This Nabal dude was such a jerk, he didn't even realize it!

"Then in the morning, when Nabal was sober, his wife told him all these things, and his heart failed him and he became like a stone" (1 Sam 25:37).

Isn't that something? Abigail calmly rehearsed the events of yesterday, and Nabal was so struck by his own stupidity, by his frighteningly close brush with death, that he had a stroke, right on the spot!

"About ten days later, the LORD struck Nabal and he died" (1 Sam 25:38).

Note that: The Lord did it, not David. *Listen friend, if you are, at this very moment, doing battle with Nabal, you need to understand something:* God can fight that battle much more effectively than you.

The music minister at our church reminded me recently of a true story that happened in his former ministry nearly 30 years ago. The minister at the time was a great fellow named Pokey Miller. And Pokey and the elders had launched a building program, one that was desperately needed to assure the ongoing growth of that fellowship. But one very vocal, very feisty man stood in stubborn opposition to the church leadership. And his obstinate objections threatened to thwart the entire project. During one Wednesday service, Pokey said that he was convinced that God was in this plan, and that God would remove any opposition to what was so clearly His will for that church. This feisty old geezer stood to his feet to object, and when he did, he had a heart attack and dropped stone dead on the floor. Great fear seized the church — and that building got built!

Now I'm not promising that if you've got an ornery husband, ten days from now, God's going to strike him dead!

What I do want you to know — is that if you'll take your cues from Him, and if you'll let Him fight your battles for you — in His good and perfect time, even the biggest mistake of your life will be made right.

Do you see how He did it for Abigail?

THE PROPOSAL

> "When David heard that Nabal was dead, he said, 'Praise be to the LORD, who has upheld my cause against Nabal for treating me with contempt. He has kept his servant from doing wrong and has brought Nabal's wrongdoing down on his own head'" (1 Sam 25:39a).

My record is unsoiled; and Nabal has gotten what he deserved. Now get this:

> "Then David sent word to Abigail, asking her to become his wife" (1 Sam 25:39b).

Get a load of how he proposed:

> "His servants went to Carmel and said to Abigail, 'David has sent us to you to take you to become his wife.' She bowed down with her face to the ground and said, 'Here is your maidservant, ready to serve you and wash the feet of my master's servants'" (1 Sam 25:40-41).

David doesn't score very high on the Don Juan Scale, does he? And yet, look at Abigail's marvelous response. Young men, that's the kind of woman you want to marry — and marry as quickly as possible. That's not subservience you are observing; that's a humble, gracious, responsive spirit. And it is in rare supply to be sure.

> "Abigail quickly got on a donkey and, attended by her five maids, went with David's messengers and became his wife" (1 Sam 25:42).

And they lived happily ever after.

Time out. It doesn't really say that, does it? No marriage is *"happily ever after."* Not even a great marriage. But because

Abigail had paid her dues, and because David had done what was right — God gave them each other, and the union that was formed was a thing of beauty.

THE PROPOSITION

A story like this is not at all difficult to apply. There's something for everyone in the story of Abigail. I find five such applications.

First, let me suggest that *DIFFERENCES BETWEEN HUSBANDS AND WIVES CAN BE A DELIGHT — THEY DON'T HAVE TO SPELL DISASTER.*

I say that because although Abigail was **"intelligent and beautiful,"** and Nabal was **"surly and mean"** it didn't automatically mean that their relationship was, therefore, a bust. On the contrary. I'm convinced that because Abigail was determined to make this thing work, and even though she got little support from her mate, these two actually had some happy times between them. They enjoyed some good history, despite their differences.

You see, contrary to popular opinion, **"one flesh"** does not mean, *"entirely alike."* No way. Every marriage I know — even the great ones — are marked by a striking, obvious diversity.

Men love the remote control; women hate the remote control. Now it's not a conscious thing — men don't go to night school in order to learn how to click through the channels! And I don't really think it's a power thing, either. Or something sexual. It's just the way we're made!

If your son belches at the evening meal, mom usually gets red-faced and chastises the poor child. Dad, also red-faced, is doing his dead-level best to choke back an approving chuckle.

Moms want kids to eat vegetables, while Dads hate eating vegetables as much as the kids.

When moms think they're lost, they pull into a gas station and ask for directions. Dads NEVER get lost.

Moms are always cold. Dads are always hot. Which is why the dirtiest half-inch in our home is that spot right under the thermostat.

And as frustrating as those differences may be, it is those differences that add spice and variety to your home. And quite often, it is those very differences that attracted you to your mate in the first place.

Listen up, all you wives who are determined to change their husbands into an image of your own making — you who have no intention of being content until you get him right where you want him.

And listen up, all you husbands who can't tolerate your wife's competence. Isn't it amazing how some men are so threatened by the fact that their wives have their own opinions — they're convinced it's wrong? They conclude it's a submission thing. They view their wives as some sort of extension of themselves, and because their "women" don't always hold to the party line — they can't handle it!

Yet the truth is, differences can be a delight! Despite the obvious differences between Abigail and Nabal, I find no hint that this woman was trying to finagle a way out of her vows. Why, she so believed that she was to stay in that marriage, that she put her own life on the line — just to save his life. Talk about delight!

Here's a second application: ***AN ANGRY SPIRIT IS ALWAYS A DESTRUCTIVE SPIRIT. A hostile heart cannot bring about the righteous life that God desires.***

I made a quick list of some of the characteristics of an angry mate. And let me say, if you are marked by two or more of these characteristics, God help the person you live with.

First, is *STUBBORNNESS*. An obstinate, headstrong spirit. It's your way or the highway, baby!

Then there's *LEGALISM*. The meticulous observance of MY regulations. It's done my way or it's wrong. And as a result, everyone who crosses me is miserable.

And how about a *RUDE AND OVERBEARING SPIRIT*?

Or an *ARGUMENTATIVE ATTITUDE*? Where, no matter what the subject you're right and everybody else is wrong. If everyone else says the sky is blue, you will argue to the death that it's really slate grey.

Then there's a *CRITICAL SPIRIT*. The intentional magnifying of the faults of the others.

Or how about an *UNFORGIVING SPIRIT*? Someone has observed that *"computers can now keep a man's every transgression recorded in a permanent memory bank, duplicating with complex programming and intricate wiring a feat his wife handles quite well without fuss or fanfare."*[25]

That's an angry spirit — and it's absolutely destructive to a relationship.

Which is why Scripture says:

"Do not be quickly provoked in your spirit, for anger resides in the lap of fools" (Eccl 7:9).

"Refrain from anger and turn from wrath. Do not fret. It only leads to evil" (Ps 37:8).

"Better a man who controls his temper than one who takes a city" (Prov 16:32).

"Everyone should be quick to listen, slow to speak, and slow to become angry, because anger does not bring about the righteous life God desires" (James 1:19-20).

No, not all anger is sin. But that's another sermon. The fact is — an angry hostile spirit *is* a tool of destruction. And if anger is raging out of control in your life? You'd better deal with it. Because the alternative is disaster.

A true story is told of a minister and his wife who were traveling by car from their home in Austin, MN, to visit their son's family in Grand Rapids, MI. Traffic, as usual, was heavy around Chicago and was backed up at one of the toll booths on the expressway.

While waiting in a long line of cars, the minister decided to kill his engine. As soon as he did so, the woman driving the car behind him began honking her horn, and honked and honked and honked.

Finally, the minister lost his temper, jumped out of his car, and yelled at the woman: *"Why don't you try blowing your horn a little bit louder?"* Then he felt this sudden rush of air-conditioning.

You see, he had forgotten that, to give himself more comfort while driving, he had unfastened the belt on his trousers. And when he jumped out of the car, he *pantsed* himself. They fell right down to his ankles. The moral of the story is this: FITS OF ANGER CAN REVEAL A LOT MORE ABOUT YOU THAN YOU WANT TO HAVE KNOWN. So deal with it.

Here's a third principle: ***THE BEST RESPONSE TO AN ANGRY SPIRIT IS WISDOM, NOT WEAPONRY.***

There's a great old fable about a lion, a donkey, and a fox. They had just finished killing all kinds of animals and prey in the wilderness, and it was time to divvy up the spoil. So the lion said to the donkey, *"Donkey, take the pile of all the killings and divide them into three equal parts."* The donkey quickly did as he was told.

Immediately, the lion pounced on the donkey and ate him up. Then he put all the piles back together and said, *"Mr. Fox, how about you dividing up the piles into two equal parts?"*

Well, the fox thought for a moment, then he reached in and took out one dead crow and put it to the side and left the rest of the pile on the other side.

The lion said, *"Mr. Fox, I can't believe how smart you are! Where did you learn how to divide so equally?"* He said, *"The donkey taught me."*

What a great parable. When you live with an angry mate, the last thing you want to do is trade firepower. To try to match your Nabal blow for blow. Now, discernment is the key. Wisdom is the only weapon that can win the battle against anger.

Wisdom is what helps you understand that countering anger with anger is counterproductive. Scripture says, **"a gentle answer turns away wrath, but a harsh word stirs up anger"** (Prov 15:1).

Wisdom is what enables you to try to understand the source of anger instead of react to the anger itself. Wisdom understands, for example, that some people lose control because of circumstances that don't even involve you. And it's in those moments that a well-timed word of comfort is just the thing to turn anger away, while an ill-timed rebuke only pours more salt in the wound. Proverbs 16:24 says, **"Pleasant words are a honeycomb, sweet to the soul and healing to the bones."**

Wisdom also helps you to know when to speak and when to be silent. Just as in the case of Abigail, there are times when the best thing you can do is hold your tongue. Psalm 141:3 says, **"Set a guard over my mouth, O LORD; keep watch over the door of my lips."** *Don't let me just spout off. Don't let me say everything that's in my heart. Don't allow me the luxury of trading insult for insult.*

Ogden Nash wrote:

> *"If you want your marriage to sizzle*
> *With love in the loving cup,*
> *Whenever you're wrong, admit it,*
> *Whenever you're right, shut up!"*

Wisdom also compels you to listen before you spout off. To listen to what the person is actually saying, not just what you think he's saying. Wisdom helps you listen just long enough to realize that you aren't the object of the anger — even though your mate may be attacking you. Scripture says: **"Like apples of gold in settings of silver is a word spoken in *right* circumstances"** (Prov 25:11, NASB).

Fourth, *THE KEY TO RESOLVING CONFLICT IS THE ABILITY TO ACCEPT YOUR MATE EVEN WHEN YOU DON'T AGREE WITH YOUR MATE.*

I think Abigail had this one nailed. She didn't say what she said about her husband because of resentment or a bitter spirit. And it wasn't gossip, either. She said what she said because it was true. She had an honest, accepting appraisal of her husband — which allowed her to realistically share her burden and not just stuff it. You see, the difference is in the motive. The difference is the attitude that is expressed. And one way to cope with an angry mate is to honestly assess the problem so that you can then accept him as he is (weakness and all), realizing that you have your share of weaknesses, too.

Fifth, and finally: *PLEASE REMEMBER THAT GOD REWARDS THOSE WHO OBEY.*

You do it right, my friend — even in the face of an angry, hostile mate — and in God's good time, your faithfulness will be more than adequately rewarded. Listen to these words:

> **"I waited patiently for the LORD; he turned to me and heard my cry. He lifted me out of the slimy pit, out of the mud and mire; he set my feet on a rock and gave me a firm place to stand. He put a new song in my mouth, a hymn of praise to our God. . . . Blessed is the man who makes the LORD his trust"** (Ps 40:1-3a, 4a).

Please understand, I don't think that means that He'll ice your husband by next Wednesday. I don't think you can necessarily plan on a funeral any time soon.

Having said that, I did happen to come across a true story that happened back in 1972. A Czechoslovakian woman named Vera Czerniak was so upset by the news her husband had betrayed her that she tried to commit suicide. She leaped from a third-story window and landed on her husband, killing him instantly. She walked away with nothing but scratches.

Now ladies, I can't promise that that's the way it's going to work for you. As far as you are concerned, the husband you have is the husband God gave you. And as imperfect as he may be, your challenge is to make the best of it. And your decision to be content in that will go a long way in determining the health and happiness of your home.

NOTES

[1] Dhammapada, source unknown.

[2] Stephen Covey, *The Seven Habits of Highly Effective People* (New York: Simon and Schuster, 1989).

[3] Spencer Marsh, *Edith the Good* (New York: Harper and Row, 1977).

[4] Ethel Barrett, *Peace & Quiet (and other Hazards)* (Old Tappan, NJ: Revell, 1980), p. 26.

[5] Lane Olinghouse, source unknown.

CHAPTER TEN

The Way Things Ought to Be
GENESIS 2:18-25

A young bride and groom had just arrived at their honeymoon cottage, and boy were they excited! They had waited for this moment of unbridled intimacy for months. It had been difficult, but they had managed to restrain themselves, saving themselves for this very, very special night. The groom went into the bathroom to change, but when he took off his socks, he remembered that he had to tell his new bride the most terrible secret of his life — *his feet stunk terribly.* He worried and fretted, but he couldn't come up with a solution, so he just went back into the bedroom and jumped in bed.

His bride went into the bathroom next, and as she was brushing her teeth, she remembered *her* horrifying secret: She had dreadfully bad breath. She didn't know what to tell her new husband, but she finally decided to just go back into the room and tell him. As she got into bed, she turned his direction, looked him squarely in the face and said, *"Darling, I have something I must tell you."*

Horrified, he looked at her and said, *"You ate my socks!?"*

Talk about disillusionment! Yet it's inevitable, isn't it? There comes a time in every marriage when love's blinders are removed, and we see our mates not as they *want* us to see them

— but as they really are. *And we don't always like what we see, do we?*

Tim Timmons maintains that there are basically three stages that most couples go through in marriage. Stage #1 is the **IDEAL.** That's when everyone is excited, when love is grand, and "our marriage is gonna be different!" But then along comes stage #2. And we move from the ideal to the **ORDEAL.** This is that time when we realize that our Prince Charming has warts, and that our Sleeping Beauty is not nearly so lovely once she wakes up. Then, far too often, along comes stage #3. That's when either one or both spouses begin looking for a **NEW DEAL.** Have you noticed that trend?

A trend which prompted one man to observe that marriage is lot like flies on a window pane: *Those who are out want in and those who are in want out!*

Perhaps you've heard the story of the cranky old woman who had died, and her body was placed in state in a casket in the back bedroom of her home. After three days of lying in state, her casket was closed, and preparations were made to carry her to the church for the funeral service. As she was being carried out, however, her pallbearers accidentally bumped the casket into a door frame, and immediately there was heard the sound of rapping from inside the casket. They opened it up, and, sure enough, she was alive! In fact, she lived for another five years. And was just as cranky as ever. Five years later, she died again and was once more placed in a casket in the back bedroom for three days. When the men prepared to carry her out this time, her husband rushed to where they were and said, *"Now you be careful of that door this time!"*

I suppose the wit has a point: *Marriage is like a hot bath — once you get used to it, it's not so hot.*

Let's face it: *Never before has marriage been so popular; never before has marriage been so perverted.* And yet, I'm not so convinced that the solution is in ditching the institution of marriage; rather it is in returning to God's original blueprint to find out how it is that marriage *ought* to be.

You see, you cannot make proper use of anything until you understand what it is made for. That's true whether we're talking snow skis or bungee cords.

I hold in my hand a felt-tip pen. It is wonderfully ideal for the purpose for which it was made. But if I try to use this felt-tip pen as a screwdriver — not only will it not accomplish that objective, but I will essentially ruin the pen for the purpose for which it was made.

So also marriage. We've practically ruined the institution because we've tried to make marriage be what marriage was never intended to be. Which is why I think it's long overdue that we open God's glove compartment and read the Owner's Manual.

So let's travel back in time to the land of Eden, the story of which, thankfully, God has faithfully saved for us in the second chapter of Genesis. And in so doing, He has preserved for us the story of how the original marital prototype was developed. But please understand, the marriage we will read about is the only IDEAL MARRIAGE that has ever been.

You may know couples who are marvelously well-adjusted to each other; you may know marriages that enjoy a wonderfully harmonious relationship. But contrary to popular opinion, THE MARRIAGE BETWEEN ADAM AND EVE WAS THE ONLY MARRIAGE IN HISTORY THAT WAS TRULY MADE IN HEAVEN. Not David and Bathsheba. Not Moses and Zipporah. Not Abraham and Sarah. No. *The first and only ideal marriage was between Adam and Eve. And I want to show you why that's the case.*

THE WAY IT USED TO BE

To do so, we need to travel back to Earth's very first week. And you will remember that throughout those first six days, God is busily creating some very wonderful things. He creates the earth and then says, **"It is good."** Then He creates some plants and says, **"It is good."** Then He forms some animals — a few fish, some birds — and then He says, **"It is good."**

Then He creates Adam. He puts Adam in the Garden, steps back, strokes His beard, and says, **"No . . . this is NOT good."** I'm not kidding! Read it for yourself:

"The LORD God said, "It is not good for the man to be alone" (Gen 2:18a).

And every man said? AMEN!

Now folks, this is a comment from the Almighty God, not some pornographic pervert. Here's Adam, with everything a guy could hope for — a good job in a great environment, perfect working conditions, great housing, no weeds to pull, super retirement benefits, great food, even a perfect relationship with God. Still, God says, *"Something's missing. Wait a minute, I got it!"*

"I will make a helper suitable for him" (Gen 2:18b).

Why didn't he just create another man? Because another man would never be suitable to meet Adam's needs. He needed a **"helper."** The word means *"corresponding to . . . "* The Hebrew literally reads, *"Answering back to . . . "* Now don't take that too literally. It's not that he needed someone to talk back to him. It means that Adam had been sending out a mating call — but no one was there to respond.

Now some folks read this and wonder why, after saying that He would make Adam a helper, God immediately asks Adam to name the animals. I'll tell you why: BECAUSE GOD WAS NOT ABOUT TO WASTE EVE. I think God gave Adam this job for two reasons: *First, to show him that every other species had a mate, except him.* And *Second, to show him that none of them would work for him*! Seriously! Why else would it say . . .

"So the man gave names to all the livestock, the birds of the air and all the beasts of the field. But for Adam no suitable helper was found" (Gen 2:20, emphasis mine).

Can you imagine? In perfect innocence, Adam is checking out the animals for a wife! He sees a giraffe and says, *"Nah, how would we ever kiss?"*

"There's an elephant. No, how would we ever hug?"

"No, not that one either. She's a dog." [Sorry!]

He went through the whole animal kingdom one and by one, and there was not one who *'corresponded to,'* who was *'suitable for'* him. I'm convinced one of the reasons God put Adam through this was so that when the young couple had their first spat, Adam wouldn't come back to God and say, *"God, this Eve-thing isn't working. How 'bout a giraffe? You know, I think it might just work."* No, because of God's divinely inspired process, Eve was not wasted. Adam was more than prepared for God's chosen *"helper."*

WHY WAS THIS MARRIAGE IDEAL? Several reasons. First, *Because God hatched Eve just for Adam.* Verse 18 says He made her **"for him."** Which obviously means that he was also made for her. She was a custom-built, flawless fit. These two corresponded to each other perfectly. Eve wasn't an assembly-line product. Adam didn't have ten finalists to choose from — God made one person ideally fitted just for him.

Look at how it happened:

"So the LORD God caused the man to fall into a deep sleep; and while he was sleeping, he took one of the man's ribs and closed up the place with flesh" (Gen 2:21).

That's the second reason this was an ideal marriage: *God made Eve from Adam's own batch.* She was, in every sense of the word, a part of Adam. Which is why they hit the ground running. They faced no adjustment period, no psychological adaptation, no emotional alteration was required — because she was taken from him, and built into a perfect counterpart to him.

"Then the LORD God made a woman from the rib he had taken out of the man, and he brought her to the man" (Gen 2:22).

That's the third reason this was an ideal marriage. *God was actively involved in matching them together.* Like no other time in history, as with no other couple who has ever lived, God brought these two together. Eve was handed by God to Adam.

How did Adam respond when he saw her? How do you think he responded? He said:

> "This is now bone of my bones and flesh of my flesh; she shall be called 'woman,' for she was taken out of man" (Gen 2:23).

Actually, that's a very tame translation. The word is actually an untranslatable Hebrew expletive: Sort of a *"WOW"* in the feminine gender. *Where have you been all my life? At last! One like myself! I'll take her, God! Wrap her up! On second thought, don't! I'll take her like she is!*

I say that because verse 25 says:

> "The man and his wife were both naked, and they felt no shame" (Gen 2:25).

Why? Because they didn't have a scratch on them, that's why. They were perfect specimens! There was no sin to hide. No shame to harbor. These two could enjoy a marvelously intimate relationship, because there was no need to cover up.

A friend of mine asked his wife recently why it is so hard for her to open up to him. Her answer is classic. She said, *"It's because I invite my company to our living room, but I invite you to my bedroom."* Now that was no problem for Adam and Eve. There was no shame. There was nothing to hide. At least until sin entered the fray. But when Eve bit that fruit — that was the end of Camelot. And from that time until this, it seems that everything about marriage has changed.

THE WAY IT OUGHT TO BE

With one major exception: God's original prescription for how marriage ought to be has NOT changed. Do you see it in verse 24? Genesis 2:24 is *the* foundational verse on marriage. It is, in every sense of the word, *HOW THINGS OUGHT TO BE.* Despite the fact that heaven no longer provides a personalized dating service, despite the fact that couples are no longer literally bone of bone and flesh of flesh, despite the fact that sin has marked our hearts and built huge walls between us — *the central truth of marriage is: although it's not perfect, it is to be permanent, and it can be a blessing.*

Now that's a tough pill to swallow, especially in the '90s, when we seem to throw away relationships with the ease of throwing away a used tissue. But God said it in Genesis, Jesus repeated it in Matthew, and Paul underscored it in Ephesians: *marriage is designed by God to operate according to THREE FUNDAMENTAL PRIORITIES.* And this is where we must begin and where we must end if we would ever know marriage as God designed it to be. Now these three principles are not multiple choice. You don't pick one and leave two. You don't pick two and leave the one you don't prefer. You pick all three and accept all three and cultivate all three — or your marriage will never be what it ought to be.

If your marriage is to be what it ought to be — **THERE HAS TO BE A LEAVING.**

"For this reason a man will leave his father and mother..."

Now that's not a reference to abandoning or forsaking your parents. It's a reminder that when you establish your new home, you are to loosen your dependency on mom and dad. Whether it's an emotional dependency or even a financial dependency — you are to **"leave"** them.

By the way, do you know why Billy Boy never married? Remember the song, *Billy Boy?* You move through the song, and you get the impression that it was because his girlfriend was just a teenager. No way. Listen:

> *"How old is she, Billy Boy, Billy Boy?*
> *How old is she, charming Billy?*
> *Three times six and four times sev'n,*
> *Twenty eight and elev'n,*
> *She's a young thing and cannot leave her mother!"*

Go ahead — do the math: 3×6 plus 4×7 plus 28 plus 11 = 85 YEARS OLD! Makes you wonder how old her mother was, doesn't it?

Now there are a lot of folks who, even though they get married, still haven't left mom and dad! But this principle is so vital that this **"leaving"** is to happen even if you plan to live under the same roof. The Bible is replete with stories of men and women who married, and yet still lived in the tent right next to mom and dad. But there still had to be a severing of the apron strings.

Take, for example, the story of Esau. Esau was a young man who didn't handle this *"leaving"* very well. He was a twin, the older of the two, and, out of rebellion, he ignored his parent's wise counsel concerning his choice of a mate. In doing so, he purposefully wreaked havoc in his home. Primarily because he did not LEAVE.

> **"When Esau was forty years old, he married Judith daughter of Beeri the Hittite, and also Basemath daughter of Elon the Hittite. They were a source of grief to Isaac and Rebekah"** (Gen 26:34-35).

Note that. Esau and his two wives were a **"source of grief"** to Esau's parents.

Why?

Because he had married not one, but TWO unbelievers!

Yeh, but even though they didn't agree with their son's sensual practice, Esau was a still grown man — and if that's the way he chose to live, at least he was married and out of the house! At least they didn't have to live with it!

Oh yes they did! You see, Esau married these two Gentile women, and then he had the audacity to move into mom and dad's basement and rub their nose in his rebellion! And it was a hell on earth for Isaac and Rebekah. I'm sure they tried to make it work, but married children just aren't meant to live with mom and dad. And it was only a matter of time before there was a blow-up!

> **"Rebekah said to Isaac, 'I'm disgusted with living because of these Hittite women. If Jacob takes a wife from among the women of this land, from Hittite women like these, my life will not be worth living'"** (Gen 27:46).

I can hear her now! *"Oi veh! I've had it up to here! If his little brother marries one like these women, it'll be the big one. I just know it!"*

Now you husbands who have lived with an hysterical wife know all too well the problem that Isaac faced. You desperately want peace in the house, so you do what Isaac did. Isaac pulled his younger son aside and gave Jacob some very helpful advice:

> "So Isaac called for Jacob and blessed him and commanded him: 'Do not marry a Canaanite woman.'
> Then Isaac sent Jacob on his way, and he went to Paddan Aram, to Laban son of Bethuel the Aramean, the brother of Rebekah, who was the mother of Jacob and Esau.
> Now Esau learned that Isaac had blessed Jacob and had sent him to Paddan Aram to take a wife from there, and that when he blessed him he commanded him, 'Do not marry a Canaanite woman,' and that Jacob had obeyed his father and mother and had gone to Paddan Aram.
> Esau then realized how displeasing the Canaanite women were to his father Isaac; so he went to Ishmael and married Mahalath, the sister of Nebaioth and daughter of Ishmael son of Abraham, in addition to the wives he already had" (Gen 28:1b, 5-9).

Now isn't that something? You think that boy wanted his parent's love? He wanted it so badly he married yet another woman! He saw that Jacob went and, in obedience to his parents, sought a wife according to their counsel. And he wanted his parents' approval too, but because of his earlier rebellion, he bought for himself even more problems. If only he had listened to his parents!

Now understand, the PRINCIPLE OF LEAVING does not insist that you ignore your parents' counsel. Not at all! Isaac and Rebekah were well within their rights to counsel their boys regarding who they should marry. And it's amazing, young people, how quickly our parents can figure out our dates — even before we figure them out. So don't ignore their godly wisdom.

But parent, never forget that your child has been given to you for a very limited period of training. And by the time your child is making decisions about who she will date and with whom she will mate, your job is, for all practical purposes, essentially complete. If you've done the job right, you've been preparing your child for mate selection from infancy. If you've waited until she's 16, it's too late. And when your child comes to you and says, *"Mom, Dad — this is the person that God wants me to marry . . . ,"* when that decision has been made, when your counsel has been given and the wedding march begins to play — THAT'S WHEN YOU ARE TO GIVE YOUR CHILD BACK TO THE SAFE-KEEPING OF GOD! *That's when you must let go!*

I can still remember my wedding day. My Dad came to me and said, *"Son, you're on your own, now. I'm here for counsel when you need it. But you won't hear it unless you ask. And if you don't make it work with Vanessa, don't come running home to us. We're moving on with our lives, Steve — and it's time for you to do the same. You're a man now. I love you, but you're on your own."*

Do I have to tell you that that was the greatest wedding gift we received? And I look forward to the day when I can give that identical speech to my son. Mom, Dad — you gotta let go!

And while we're at it, parents, YOU'D BETTER ACCEPT THAT NEW IN-LAW. Your acceptance means more to your adult child than you will ever dream. Don't make the new kid on the block earn your affection. Give it freely. Take him in. Draw her in. In the Wyatt household, I'm convinced that if our marriage ever dissolved, my parents would choose Vanessa over me. And that's the way it ought to be in your home, too!

So have you "left" your original home? If not, I have some words of counsel for you.

First, STOP QUOTING MOM AND DAD. Stop saying, *"Honey, mom always did it this way."* Or, *"Dear, dad always did his own plumbing!"* Or, *"Why do you go to Grease Monkey? Daddy always changed his own oil!"* *"Daddy always said this, Momma always did that. . . ."* You hear that long enough and you want to say, **"Well then, why don't you just go live with daddy and momma?"** REALLY!

The Way Things Ought to Be

Leave mom and dad out of your relationship . . . OK? Let your husband fix it — HIS way! Let your bride make it her way! I can still remember several years ago, suggesting that Vanessa call my Mom and get her recipe for potato salad. I had no idea that someone could hold such firm convictions about chunks or mashed! But thank the Lord, I'm a quick study. I realized early on that it's a lot easier on me and my marriage to just eat whatever she makes.

This principle of leaving is so important that it's actually mentioned to a couple who had nobody to leave from! *Have you ever thought about that?* There was no one else around! But God knew that, in time, Adam's job would start demanding more and more of his time, that Cain and Abel would start dominating Eve's every waking moment, and that Adam and his buddies would want to play cards over at the Canaanite Cafe three nights a week, AND IN GOD'S OMNISCIENT WISDOM, HE LAID DOWN A DIVINE PRINCIPLE FOR MARITAL MAINTENANCE — in advance.

The principle? NOTHING, ABSOLUTELY NOTHING, IS TO TAKE PRECEDENCE OVER YOUR RELATIONSHIP WITH YOUR MATE. And when it does, you are in clear violation of the first fundamental priority of marriage.

But there's a second principle: If your marriage is to be what it ought to be — **THERE ALSO HAS TO BE A CLEAVING.**

"For this reason a man will leave his father and mother . . . and be united to his wife" (Gen 2:24b, emphasis added).

The old King James version put it like this: **"he shall cleave unto his wife."** Now let's make this clear — this has no relationship whatever to a meat cleaver. Ever since Lorena Bobbitt and O.J. Simpson, we expositors have to be extremely careful to explain our meaning on such things. The word "cleave" has nothing to do with slicing and dicing. The word "cleave" means *"to cling or glue to something. To keep close to something and remain bonded to it."*

This same word is used in 2 Kings 5:27 to describe leprosy which *clings* to the body. And again in Job 19:20, describing bones that *cling* to the skin. And in Ezekiel it describes scales *clinging* to a fish. Now, scales cling to a fish and bones to a body and leprosy to skin — because they are joined as one. They are merely different parts of the same thing!

And that's the point: God, at the very inception of marriage, said: THIS THING IS FOR LIFE! The marital bond is a permanent, lasting, never-to-be-severed bond.

Now I realize, some people hear that and they say, *"Well, man's just not built that way."* They say that man is not *"monogamous by nature."* He can't just stay with one woman. Have you ever heard that? I think it's probably true. But I also think it's irrelevant.

You look at nature, and a bull is delighted to service a whole barnyard of cows. That's his nature. A dog isn't any better, and we all know about rabbits. Maybe it **is** nature to pursue multiple relationships.

The problem is: The Christian believes that nature is not always right! *That nature, in fact, is fallen!* You see, Adam and Eve didn't struggle in this regard because their nature was like God's! Our nature is in stark rebellion against God! But rather than just shrug our shoulders and throw in the towel, we who are disciples of Christ are in the lifelong process of learning how to say "NO" to nature.

Now even the heathen believe in saying "no" to nature. At least in some ways. For example, I've never seen a bull in a bathroom. Nature calls and he obeys — no matter where he may be. Human beings have learned to wait a little while, unless they're in church — then they are obligated to obey immediately.

So maybe it **is** true: PERHAPS MARITAL COMMITMENT *IS* ABSOLUTELY CONTRARY TO THE LAWS OF NATURE!

So what? The fact is, when you stood before the Lord, whether it was in a beautiful house of worship or a justice of the peace, and when you said, *"I take you to be my wedded wife, to have and to hold from this day forward, for better or for worse, for richer or for poorer, in sickness and in health, to love and to cherish until death do us part,"* you were making a covenant with the future. A vow to your God! A vow of permanence!

But Steve! Those vows aren't natural! Besides, we just say them so we can get married in a church. We don't really mean it. After all, the real culprit is society. I mean, society forces people to get married.

Oh really? Have you ever seen society do that? Have you ever seen a couple of parents or some wicked preacher chain two people together and force them to make those horrible commitments to each other? NO! That's not the way it happens.

Let me tell you the way it happens: Two people meet and fall in love. And they start making all kinds of ridiculous promises to each other: *I will swim the seven seas, I will cross the widest ocean, I will climb the highest mountain, I will lay down my life for you . . . BABE!* Gag! When love hits, it's like a drunken stupor — you go blind, you lose your mind, and you're like a freight train running down the mountainside — no brakes and no way to get off! And parents and preachers and friends are running alongside screaming, *"Get off! Get off while you can!"* But do you listen? You don't listen. You smile, you swoon, you drool, you purr — and then you drag each other into some church building, walk down an aisle in a narcotic-like trance and promise hair-raising oaths to each other! *"Do you?" "I do." "Do you?" "I do."* And then you kiss, and nobody can pull you apart! You go to the reception and you're the first ones out the door — and everybody's glad because all that lollygagging was making us sick anyway.

NOW — DID SOMEBODY MAKE YOU DO THAT? Who was so cruel as to force you into that kind of idiocy?

But then a few months pass, and the scales start to fall from your eyes. You were blind, but now you see! And he realizes she's not a fairy princess after all. In fact, she's terrifyingly similar to his mother-in-law! Oh what a tragedy of unparalleled proportions! And she discovers that he's got some ugly habits that just drive her up a wall! And they both discover, doggone it, that there are a lot of good-looking women and kind, compassionate men out there! And I don't know how it happened, but, preacher, I'm bored!

And suddenly, the chains and the ropes that they so willingly tied around themselves seem too tight, too constraining, too binding! And all they want to do is get out!

I had a fellow once say to me, *"Steve, I'm gonna trade my woman in on a newer model. Mine's gettin' a little frumpy and well-traveled."*

I said, *"And just how did she get that way? By bearing your children and putting up with you? Do you have any idea what kind of a trip that's been for her?"*

Maybe your wife IS aging on the outside, but she's also becoming more and more delightful on the inside. And God says, **"Remember the wife of your youth. Keep your marriage covenant. Cleave to that union."** (See Malachi 2:13-16.)

Finally: If your marriage is to be what it ought to be — **THERE ALSO HAS TO BE A WEAVING.**

"For this reason a man will leave his father and mother and be united to his wife . . . and they will become one flesh" (Gen 2:24c).

Note that: They **"become"** one flesh. They weave themselves into each other's life. And that's a process, not an instantaneous event. *One flesh* doesn't happen just because the preacher says, "I now pronounce you husband and wife;" it doesn't happen when you sign the legal documents; it doesn't happen at the hotel ten miles down the road. It is a lifelong process. And it's built upon the previous two principles. Only as you make room in your life for your mate can you weave your life into hers. And only as you make a covenant vow to cleave unto your wife will you be willing to so blend your heart with hers that you become, in every sense of the word, a TEAM!

Rodney Dangerfield says: *"We sleep in separate rooms, we have dinner apart, we take separate vacations – we're doing everything we can to keep our marriage together."*

The Way Things Ought to Be

Henny Youngman says: *"Some people ask the secret of our long marriage. We take time to go to a restaurant two times a week. A little candlelight, dinner, soft music and dancing. She goes Tuesdays, I go Fridays."*

No! That's not weaving! That's not building a team! Weaving takes place when I accept you for both your strengths and your weaknesses. And I see God's obvious wisdom in joining us together in such a way that my weaknesses are built up by your strengths, and your weaknesses are sustained by my strengths. Team is what happens when I decide to cooperate with you, not compete against you.

I love football. And I often think of life in a football kind of imagery. But you don't have to be a football fan to know this: YOU DON'T TACKLE THE GUYS WHO WEAR THE SAME COLOR UNIFORM. Right? Just imagine the Dallas Cowboys in a crucial game situation. The offense is within seven yards of the end zone, just about to score the go-ahead touchdown with barely two minutes left in the game. Now do you know what would happen if Troy Aikman hands the ball to Emmitt Smith, who fumbles it away and the Cowboys lose the game? Practically everybody on the team will come by, slap him on the bottom and say, *"Tough luck, Emmitt. We'll get 'em next time. It's alright. We'll get it back!"* Can you imagine what would happen if they said: *"Thanks a lot, superstar!" "Is that why they give you the big bucks, so you can lose the ball for us?" "That was a big help, Smith!"*

I'm thinking of the legacy of Leon Lett, an interior lineman on the Cowboys' stingy defensive squad. On Thanksgiving Day, November 28, 1993, Leon Lett committed one of the dumbest plays in NFL history. He touched the ball following a blocked field goal in the final seconds of the game, allowing the Miami Dolphins to kick again for a 16-14 victory.

That happened a mere ten months following another Lett blunder in the previous year's Super Bowl. What happened in that game? He recovered a fumble and was rumbling toward a certain touchdown when he decided to celebrate early. And when he did, Buffalo's Don Beebe caught him from behind, stripped him of the ball and nullified a sure seven points.

Now you would think that after two nationally-televised blunders that Lett's teammates would be a little irritated. Well, if that's what you think, you are wrong. Troy Aikman, a couple of nights later on the Tonight Show, called Leon one of the Cowboys' *"great ball players."* And Coach Jimmy Johnson was quoted as saying, *"Leon Lett is an integral part of our team."*

That's what I mean by TEAM, folks. Even dumb football players realize that you have to pull together when things are falling apart. That you're either on your teammate's back or you're on his team — you can't have it both ways!

The WEAVING PRINCIPLE demands that you do the same with your mate. That you accept your mate — warts and all, mistakes and all, foibles and all — and that you enter fully into his/her world and blend yourself completely as his/her partner.

The best illustration I know of this is a story called: **THE TEN-COW WIFE.** I don't know who told this story first, but it's a great one.

Many years ago, on the island of Oahu in the Hawaiian Islands, the people observed a most unusual custom. A prospective husband paid a family a certain number of cows for their daughter to become his wife. The standard price? Three cows for a bride. If she was a particularly wonderful catch, she might actually fetch four cows. There was a rumor, though it was unconfirmed, that at some time in the distant past, one young damsel had actually fetched the astronomical price of five cows.

On the island lived a man with two daughters. The older one was what we would call a "reject." She was not at all a desirable candidate for marriage. Her father had despaired of ever getting three cows for her and had long ago decided that he would gladly accept a two-cow offer; and if the suitor was a good bargainer, he would even let her go for one cow. The truth is, if push came to shove, in order to marry her off, old Dad would have gladly let her go for no cows.

The Way Things Ought to Be

Such was not the case with her younger sister, a ravishing beauty with charm and character, so old Dad knew he would easily rid himself of her and was not concerned in the least about her future.

When Johnny Lingo, the richest man on the island, came calling on this household, everyone knew he was coming to see the younger daughter. To everyone's astonishment—and to Dad's delight—he came calling on the older daughter. Old Dad just about flipped with joy! Since Johnny was the richest man, as well as the most generous man on the island, old Dad knew that Johnny would, in his generosity, be delighted to give at least the standard three-cow price. He even let his imagination get the better of him and thought that since Johnny was both generous and wealthy, he might even go four cows. Then his imagination turned to insanity, and he figured maybe Johnny would even go for the rumored price of five cows. You can imagine his delight when Johnny came to claim his bride and brought ten cows with him! Old Dad almost had a heart attack! He quickly called the tribal chief to perform the ceremony before Johnny changed his mind, died suddenly, or regained his senses.

In those days, a standard honeymoon lasted one year, but when you have a ten-cow bride, you obviously don't take a standard three-cow honeymoon. So bride and groom set off for parts unknown with the announced intention of a full two-year honeymoon. When the day arrived for the return of the bride and groom, a lookout was posted on the edge of the village with instructions to sound the call as Johnny and his bride first came into sight.

Shortly after daylight the call was sounded: "Here comes a couple!" Naturally, everyone wanted to know: "Is it the bride and groom?" He answered that he thought so, but wasn't sure. He recognized Johnny, but he wasn't so sure about the girl. Something about her was familiar, and yet, she was beautiful — graceful, poised, confident, and self-assured. As the couple drew closer, they could see she was truly the same girl. But she had changed. Her beauty, charm, competent bearing, and poise were obvious, even to the most casual observer. And those who looked closely thought Johnny Lingo had gotten a bargain by paying "only" ten cows.

I know some who read this might dismiss it as legend, but the reality is the Johnny Lingo story has happened, not once in the long ago on a distant island, but thousands of times all over the world. Think of what Johnny's action did for that woman. His acceptance of her, his willingness to attribute to her great value, his commitment to weaving himself into her life made that one-cow, homely girl into a ten-cow wife! And it still can happen to this day.

Men, if you want a ten-cow wife, you gotta' start treating her like a ten-cow wife. And you need to attribute ten-cow value and respect to her.

Now that's one tough assignment, don't you agree? Vanessa, my wife, is without doubt, the strength of our relationship. She is a reserved and very self-sufficient woman. But she also is, in every sense of the word, a ten-cow wife. But the truth is, I have the toughest time telling her that. I'll stand up in front of the church I serve and tell them. I'll even put it in print and tell you, but it's a horrendous battle for me to willingly attribute to her the value that I place in her.

But as difficult as it is, I have found these words to be true: Zig Ziglar says, *"If you treat your wife like a thoroughbred, she will seldom act like a nag."*

And ladies, it works the same way for your husbands (actually it works even better). Ed Young says, *"Man does not live by bread alone; he needs to be "buttered up" from time to time."* Treat him like a *champ,* and you'll never wind up with a "chump!"

Goethe expressed it this way: *"If you treat a man as he is, he will stay as he is. If you treat him as if he were what he ought to be and could be, he will become that bigger and better man."* That's WEAVING, and it is an absolute imperative if your marriage will ever be what it ought to be.

THE WAY TO GET THERE

Great stuff, Steve — but how do I translate it into my WIFE? I mean, my LIFE? Here's two suggestions for doing just that.

Number one, **YOU MUST ACCEPT THE FACT THAT YOUR MARRIAGE WILL NEVER BE PERFECT.** The only ideal marriage in human history was Adam and Eve's. And even they blew it. Don't forget that. Even the most successful unions know times of breakdown, doubt, disillusionment, anger, distress, and conflict. That's what this book has been all about.

But that reality doesn't have to mean that the union cannot work! I say that because I've had people come to me and say, *"Steve, we've got problems in our marriage!"* And they seem genuinely shocked about it. And I want to say, *"OK, what's your point?"* I mean, after all, you're an imperfect person, right? And you're married to yet another imperfect person, right? And you expected no problems? *Yeh, but she wasn't that way when I married her!* So, you made her that way, right! *A . . . a . . . oh!*

So what are you going to do? Focus on your assets or your liabilities? Are you going to rivet your attention on the problems or on the potential?

Which brings me to my second suggestion: **YOU MUST REALIZE THAT SUCCESS IN MARRIAGE IS NOT SO MUCH IN FINDING THE RIGHT MATE, AS IT IS IN BEING THE RIGHT MATE.**

You may think you married a dud — have you ever looked in the mirror? The truth is, you married over your head.

And even if you *did* marry the wrong person, you can treat her like the right person and make that union work! Just as you can marry the right person but treat him wrong — and the whole deal can come crashing in at your feet.

A few years ago, someone wrote Dear Abby: *"Dear Abby, I'm single; forty years old; and I'd like to meet a man about the same age who has no bad habits."*

Abby replied, *"So would I!"*

Give it up, friend. It is far more important for you to be the right person than it is for you to marry the right kind of person. Let's face it: Every *Behind the Tent Flaps* marriage has its moments. But God's way is a better way.

> *"For this reason*
> *a man will leave his father and mother*
> *and be united to his wife,*
> *and they will become one flesh."*

About the Author

Stephen T. Wyatt received his B.A. and M.Min. degrees from Kentucky Christian College. Steve has been the Senior Minister for Crossroads (formerly Cullen Avenue) Christian Church in Evansville, Indiana since 1981. The congregation has grown from 200 to over 2200 in attendance. A record attendance of nearly 5,000 celebrated Christ's resurrection at a local basketball arena on Resurrection Sunday in 1996. Steve is the principal teacher for the tape ministry, "The Cutting Edge."

Previously he served as Youth Minister for Central Church of Christ in Portsmouth, Ohio and Senior Minister for Northwest Avenue Church of Christ in Tallmadge, Ohio. Steve serves on the board of directors for TEAM Expansion Ministries and as a member on the continuation committee for the North American Christian Convention.

The author has received several honors, among which are: Outstanding Young Men of America, 1981; Outstanding Young Minister in America, 1989; Outstanding Achievement in Ministry, 1992; and membership in Delta Epsilon Chi, the honor society of the American Association of Bible Colleges.

He has authored *A Portrait of Jesus* published by College Press and co-authored *Claiming Your Place: How to Find Where You Fit in the Life of the Church* published by Standard Publishing. Steve has also published several articles in *The Christian Standard*, *The Lookout*, *Modern Maturity* and *Hoosier Parent*. He has written and designed several Equipping Courses including "Discovery"—an eight-week course on basic doctrine, "Celebration of Marriage"—an eight-week marriage enrichment course, "Plan A, There Is No Plan B"—a ten-week course for lay-evangelism, and "First Steps"—a how-to course on church involvement.

Steve Wyatt is a preacher's kid (born in Gallipolis, Ohio to Thomas and Eleanor Wyatt) turned preacher who would like his kids to remember his laughter more than his preaching. He also married a preacher's kid who declared she'd never marry a preacher. (Steve hopes she hasn't regretted her change of heart.) His infectious love for the Word of God, combined with an unswerving commitment to its practical application, makes the message he delivers refreshingly authentic and helpful to many.